TOM KOVAC

Architectural Monographs No 50

TOM KOVAC

A.D. ACADEMY EDITIONS

Acknowledgements

To Elana, for her love, inspiration, and being a child!

To all the special human beings that I encountered along the journey, for your care and belief. Thank you for your support and encouragement in the darkest of hours.

Photographic credits: all photographs are © Trevor Mein, except those of the Gibbs Church conversion which are © Francesca Malley.

COVER: Urban Attitude, Melbourne, 1996
FRONTISPIECE: Zucchini Sofa, 1991, yellow neoprene, designed by Tom Kovac for the Succhi shop in Melbourne

Architectural Monographs No 50
First published in Great Britain in 1998 by
ACADEMY EDITIONS

A division of
JOHN WILEY & SONS LTD
Baffins Lane
Chichester
West Sussex PO19 1UD

ISBN 0-471-97749-7

Other Wiley Editorial Offices
New York • Weinheim • Brisbane • Singapore • Toronto

Printed and bound in Singapore

Contents

Sapore Restaurant, Melbourne, 1995

Introduction

Leon van Schaik

A white enigma attaches itself to the work of Tom Kovac. Critics read worlds into the enticing voids. John Andrews has previously written of the work's 'intimate immensity':[1] The original size of Kovac's drawings fit in the palm of the hand. The ease and fluidity of line stems from the fingers and the wrist (not from the elbow, as with the lines drawn on a parallel motor machine or with a T-square). These drawings (are) then mechanically enlarged and plotted for the builder. Full size lines are drawn on site, on walls. This necessitate(s) constant site visits and adjustments. The space (is) developed in a totally three-dimensional manner, rather than in response to an elevated plan.

I will return to Andrews' observations about the drawings; they become crucial evidence in the case of the 'enigma'. In this monograph (pp14-15) Andrews elaborates: 'The shifting vanishing points, blurred horizon lines, and erased corners are all techniques born of the interior.' Andrews' critical position shifts seamlessly from holding the work in the palm of his hand to 'being within' a sea shell picked up on a beach. Experiencing this simultaneous duality in Kovac's buildings has led me to write of his work as an architecture of the 'third term', an architecture in the surface.

Peter King's critique (pp16-17) likens the work to a modernist mirror swallowing what it has seen. In a telling phrase he writes that Kovac 'draws in'. For King this practice consists of 'a repertoire of hidden and hiding geometries and optics shoring up or down a Romantic abyss'. This is a long way from the cool admiration evoked in the Peter Pan realm of the shell on the beach, picked up and engaged in innocent reverie.

An altogether less child-like force captures the attention of other critics. Aaron Betsky (pp18-19) argues that the logic of the work 'derives to a large degree from its programmes, which up until now have been for retail stores, restaurants, clubs and private homes'. This is not a value-free process: it is 'fixing the flows of capital into blobs'. Betsky transfers the intimacy from the act of 'building' to the act of 'dressing' – 'White, curved and rounded, it surrounds you, threatening to suffocate you with its surfeit of form. This is architecture that strikes a pose ... thus the architect is a dresser, working with a space as if it were a beautiful model or an actor full of effect.' For Betsky another more intrusively intimate 'hands-on' practice is envisaged, 'both familiar and strangely, sensuously, like some half-remembered embrace. It brings the body back into the city'. We can understand the critic's insistence on a lineage that includes Nigel Coates. The architect's vision seems to displace our everyday world. There is anecdotal evidence that his clients form visceral attachments to their houses.[2] Seemingly they take on deep significances for their owners, to the extent that they deny the importation of the accumulated clutter of previous lifetimes. These works replace life, creating new personal histories, in which – as often as not – the architect is ultimately the intruder. I have written of the decolonising effect of this phenomenon, and Betsky has previously written that this architecture is a 'slow motion version of the hectic dance of differences that make up quotidian reality ... a stand-in for sex'. Disturbed by a reverie in which he traces the fragments of past architectures through his finger tips as he (metaphorically) runs his hands over the walls of Kovac's caverns, he feels disconcertedly that here 'history repeats itself ... as a pose'.

King observes that repetition is a characteristic of 'saturated Romanticism', a practice 'in which the argument for a Romantic novel/poem is another Romantic novel/poem'. A certain *mittel europa* sensibility seems to emerge in this discourse. Georgi Stanishev (pp20-23) asks : 'What is the general type of artistic consciousness to which Kovac's poetics belong?' Kovac unveils 'the energetic fields as the immanent part of a poetic reality'. 'Sensitivity to the natural world and its energies places the works of Tom Kovac within the Romantic tradition', constructing 'a vision of the poet/architect as an individual who is able to establish an intuitive correlation between the world and his own mental universe'.

Constructing the vision of an architect, Stanishev accurately pinpoints much that Kovac projects through the form of his practice. He scorns the notion that architecture is a 'service industry'. In Kovac's view, the architect seeks a synthesis of 'correct' form that Stanishev argues expresses the clients' circumstances as resonances in the architect's art. Betsky's comparison with the practice of the couturier repays a fuller examination. That Kovac's projection of his vision of practice pervades critical space is not an accident. Like Le Corbusier, he has a pamphleteer's cunning sense of how to engage the interest of the world in his work. He seeks out the like-minded, exhibits their work, arranges lectures for them, and places his work in the context of that of others he admires.

We are, however, in error if we believe that this is a 'boutique sensibility', and a practice limited to retail stores, restaurants, clubs and private homes. The realm of intimate immensity is a scaleless world in which daydreaming transforms salt cellars into temples. Kovac's Museum of Victoria design expresses in two equal and entwined forms a desire for reconciliation at the scale of the State, while the Federation Square design reveals that his architectural reach far outstretches the boutique. Here the city is lapped by a 'wave' from the same beach that the shells come from, but this is Tsunami not

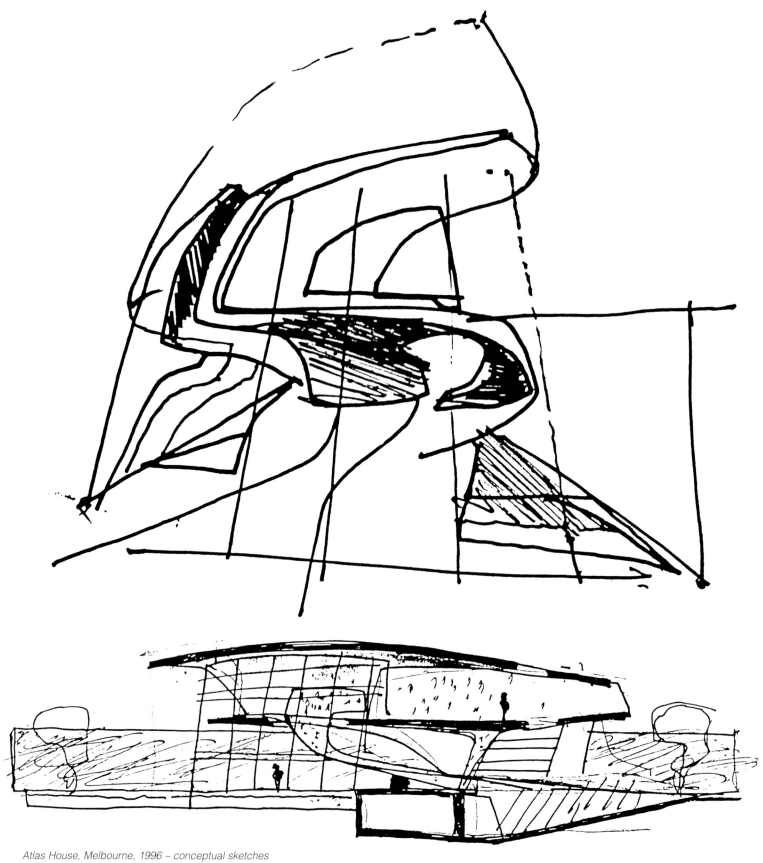

Atlas House, Melbourne, 1996 – conceptual sketches

Gucci. These works express social intent – King's 'immanence of *architecture parlante*' arises from an examination of these works. They perch perilously between immense intimacy and the large, late excesses of Konstantin Melnikov.[3] The issue of whether their surface can be realised in such a way that our reveries remain detached and transferable (and thus free of Melnikovian pathos) is one of the questions that the future tectonics of these (unbuilt/how buildable?) large projects pose. The computational power that has enabled an exploration of the mathematics of 'chaos' underpins the fluid spatiality of Kovac's work in ways that were not available to Frederick Kiesler, whose imagination was bounded by the medium of clay. Andrews' suggestion that these are spaces generated from 'the interior' defines a difference between Barbara Hepworth's sculpting and Kovac's spatial imagining. I believe that suppressing the means to the surface – as the finished drawings of these large projects seem to do – will render the architecture mute, engendering a thickness analogous to the leathery skin of Michelangelo's slaves. The future of this practice lies in an articulation of the armature that supports the 'third term' surface that is this architecture's contribution to the new.

As in the 1950s General Motors advertisement from *National Geographic*, we fantasise that we can hold a car cupped in our hands, and then drive in it – so protected – through a blizzard. This very simultaneity that makes it impossible to incorporate either carving or modelling into our mental space and causes us to experience a spatiality of the present is, I believe, behind the continuing fascination that outstrips the architect's own written theorising. These are works that engage and compel without overt literary or symbolic coding, and yet they seem to release a resonance with our ontological understandings of space; understandings that emanate from our deeply internalised histories in space – particularly at an eidetic level. I hope to suggest how this occurs as a consequence of the creation of a spatiality of the immediate present, a present that can only be accessed as we remove ourselves from the omnipresent mechanics of mundane intellectual activity and engage in reveries unloosed by this architecture.

I will now turn to the drawings themselves for evidence of Kovac's unbuilt intent. In *Why Architects Draw* Edward Robbins interviews Peter Rice, who observes: 'architects are what I would call second-order draftsmen, just like engineers are second-order mathematicians … (drawing) is not a necessary element in architecture, as it is in art.'[4] Nonetheless, 'An architect's drawing is what he wants to do. It actually ties him down.' Rice hopes for a less drafted way of working, a longer period of more tentative discourse than is presently 'good' practice, 'fixed' drawing that becomes an *idée fixe*, robbing the architecture of the depth that would come from a longer period of openness to the problem/opportunity. I believe that Kovac's drawings exhibit certain in-built hesitancies that are clues to the realisation of the large-scale work that is yet to come.

There are four broad catergories of drawing employed in Kovac's practice. Two of these – the single-weight line plans and sections, and the wire frame and pixilated three-dimensional studies – enhance the enigma of the architect's intention. They slow down the process, serving as delaying tactics interposed between the designer and the design, and (differently) between the designer and the client, the designer and the public authority. They are abstracted from the occluded atmosphere of architectural intentions that the originating 'quick' drawings exude. The final drawings are 'documentation' in a traditional sense; the radical nature of the construction process is revealed only in captions that enjoin the builder to read them in conjunction with the computer-generated positioning information: 'Provide unfaltered curve to penetration as shown in section. Refer CAD drawings for dimensioning.' (Sapore Restaurant.)

The single-weight line drawings throw certain controlling oppositions into relief without in any way depicting the spatial consequences of these tensions. The Succhi shoe shop plans show a thrusting form generated by a concavity on its head. Sections of the Capital nightclub are throated as if controlling flows of a viscous substance, while the plan oozes around into a globular conclusion. The stark mandala-like quality of the most abstract Sapore drawings won over both the local authority and the building owner. The latter arrived on site one day to find the first floor of the building being demolished. With a cry of rage he rushed at the architect declaring that this gutting of his building had ruined him. The project architect, Anthony Battersby (a body-builder whose own curves seemed to swell with that of the architecture he brought into being), stopped him, picked him up, placed him on a pile of bricks, and invited him to make a calmer assessment of the situation. The distressed owner had read the drawn lines as inscriptions in the plaster, not as holes in the floor. Kovac acknowledges the usefulness of such confusions, and then justifies them. After all, does the building owner not in fact have a higher value property as a result of the architect's interventions? And would he ever have acquiesced in his own enrichment if he had known what the architectural intentions were before he could see them in the flesh?

Anthony Battersby, Denis Daniels and Cassandra Fahey labour for long hours to turn Kovac's fast drawings into these second-order

Pless House, Melbourne, 1996 – detail of sheet of conceptual drawings

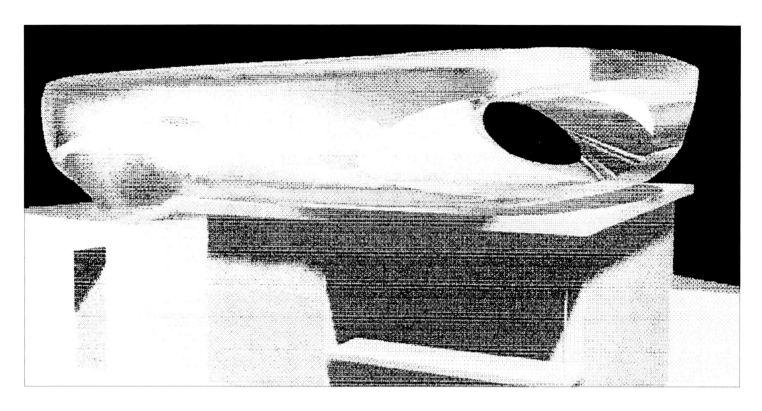

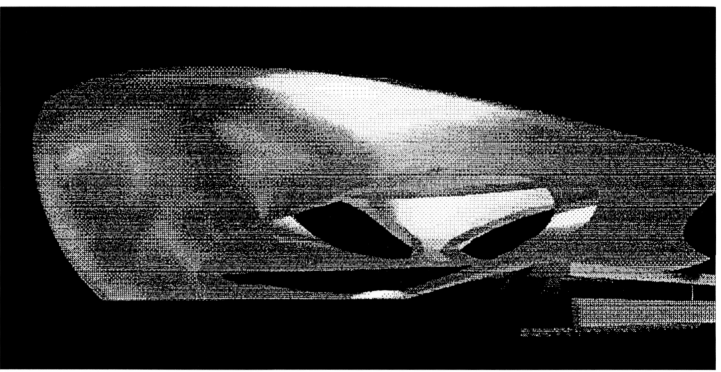

Pless House, Melbourne, 1996 – computer-generated studies of form

documents. Wire frames project skins within the orthogonal, legally-determined frames of a house extension. The new presses up against the 'staid' colonial legitimacy that has frustrated expression of a local experience of spatiality.[5] In this abstract rendering, we read objects – space vehicles perhaps – rather than the space created. The architect sees what he has wrought dispassionately, at a distance, as by other hands. He can cut himself away from the languid pleasures of the fast drawings, and see through to the finished space. Perhaps this form of reflection, from the quick and intuitive to the dispassionate and back again, has always been part of good architectural practice. Specialist ateliers now offer this feedback in startling detail to architects who previously may have been happy to rely on a simple progression from second-order drawing to model to artist's rendering.[6] Kovac's practice, like most serious architectural practices, has always embodied this checking system in its four kinds of drawing hierarchy, and the way in which it is used.

The pixilated rendering makes the forms even more ethereal, one can almost see them spin around in the designer's mind's eye, as the critical 'unfaltered curve' is sought out, interrogated, fixed. These depersonalised images turn the feverishly drawn field of imaginings into objects of contemplation, spinning timelessly out there, away from the land.

While Peter Rice argued that the problem with drawing is that it weds architects to their first idea, I believe that it lies in beginning with slow drawings, or not fully reading the first, most highly integrated, fast drawings. Kovac does not begin with slow drawings. In his case it is worth asking what information is not travelling from the fast to the slow?

There is plenty of evidence in the sketches of arrows that tease out the visual interconnectedness of different volumes in plan and section. There are rapid space-filling scrawls that create the field of the plan and tentacle-like sections in which curves are sought out or positioned. Most significant, I believe, are the readings that can be made of the density of the atmosphere that the architecture inhabits. There is a direct correlation between the originating marks and the experience of physical form even when the drawings are conveying the physical requirements for matter-of-fact construction to disintegrated parties. Meanwhile, the expressive charge of the origination remains an emotion that is implicit until released on site in a delayed manner when the last painter's can has been removed, and the client discovers that the collections of their previous lives cannot be accommodated in this realised dream of the new.

There is also, in these nervous originations, a clue to the less than enigmatic constructive tensions of making the works. These flecks, dots and huntings all seem to indicate where the work is to be attached, hung, draped. It is the expression of these forces that currently fails the translation from fast drawing to slow; it is these forces that are suppressed.

I have imagined teams of artisans applying thick gesso to the armature of the drawings. The actual means of translating the drawings into substance is a problem for those who have not experienced the work at first hand. The bending and folding of gypsum sheets held in position at critical points belies the photographic suggestion of solidity. But this sense of weight is not without substance in our actual relationship to the built forms, except where acute angles and external plays of light reveal ripples in surfaces that should have all the solidity of the externally conceived, painstakingly graded, solid-clay models of motorcar stylists. Once inside, we accept the illusion of substance because the light reveals only the lines of intention that are discovered in the fast drawings; and the curves flow obediently about these as force fields generated by that crucial attachment armature.

Where King states that 'in Kovac's work the lack is of matter and the cry is for it,' I believe that he points also to my contention that this work would benefit from an explicit revealing of the armature. Once this is seen, the full range of the architect's system of conceiving and creating space comes into focus. The third term is experienced as an active diaphragm between the inhabitable space and the intuited mathematics of the armature. Atmospheric thickening, light and the play of light and sound then convert this skin into space-enfolding matter that seems as dense as its thickest coil.

Stevie Smith wrote my favourite literary description of returning from the wars of everyday life to a familiar secure space, telling of a stone house from which winds can be watched without being heard:

> And you go in through the gate of the wall, and you shut it behind you, and you go up the pathway that is bordered by trees all blown one way in spite of the wall, and so you come to the heavy door that has a stone porch, that has steps leading up to it, and you unlock the door and you shut the door behind you, and bolt it, and inside there is a wide stone hall and lights hanging down perfectly steady. Though the wind is now roaring around the house … [7]

Kovac's space allows us to watch light and its incremental waxing and waning without the interference of the visual coding that diverts our everyday attention from these basic phenomena of the universe.

Leon van Schaik is an architect and urban designer. He is Dean of the Department of the Constructed Environment at the Royal Melbourne Institute of Technology, Australia.

Notes

1   The term comes from Gaston Bachelard, *The Poetics of Space*, Beacon Press (Boston), 1969.

2   Related by landscape designer Catherine Stutterheim, who has often worked with Tom Kovac.

3   S Frederick Starr, *Melnikov: Solo Architect in a Mass Society*, Princeton Architectural Press (New York), 1978.

4   Edward Robbins, *Why Architects Draw*, MIT Press (Cambridge, Mass), 1994, pp190-91.

5   Aaron Betsky's description of the colonising grid.

6   Ateliers such as that of John Gullings in Melbourne.

7   Stevie Smith, *Novel on Yellow Paper*, Jonathan Cape (London), 1936.

Erasing the Corner

John Andrews

When I first arrived in Australia to work at the Royal Melbourne Institute of Technology in 1990, I was introduced to Tom Kovac's work. Still with jet-lag after an eventful flight from London through a thunderstorm, I was welcomed at a place called 'The Cherry Tree'. The streets were wet from the storm and the shiny roads and pavements reflected the deep red light from a neon sign above the entrance. Once a hotel, it carries a reputation for being the rendezvous for a renowned Richmond gang at the turn of the century. It is situated in what was then a tough industrial area: long blank factory walls, tall dark chimneys, railway cuttings, iron bridges and empty car parks make up the urban landscape surrounding this corner site. On entering 'The Cherry Tree' the landscape hardly changed, the walls were kept plain with rust-coloured stained plaster and the space felt lofty and untouched. It was dark with just the necessary lighting behind the bar and above the pool table. A narrow passage away from the bar passed alongside a flight of stairs into a large cavernous space designed for performance and eating. This was where the carved epicentre expressed itself to the point of excess, and this was where Tom's future began.

Some six years later, with several substantial projects built and some new ones underway, it is possible to trace a line through his short but prolific story.

Whilst writing an article for *Architecture Australia*, I met Tom and saw some of his early sketches, detail drawings and models. I was struck by the ease with which his miniaturised curve (drawn rough) was translated to the third dimension and thereby built full-size. Hardly any of the fluidity evident in the sketches is lost in the making.

Like many of the designers graduating in the eighties, Tom was launched into a fertile world; commissions were not too difficult to attain in Melbourne at that time. Design was respected as an indication of taste. Retail was unashamedly bold, taking under its wing graphic designers, industrial designers and fashion designers, as well as architects and interior designers. By the nineties the economic swell retracted leaving in its wake the flotsam and jetsam of a decade of rampant consumerism, but also some spatial experiments which have since grown into fully resolved buildings. This is not without precedent: Hans Hollien's candle shop in Vienna and Peter Wilson's Blackburn house in London come immediately to mind as small-scale, highly influential prototypes and models for much larger and more complex buildings to follow. In this respect the architecture becomes autobiographical where certain details are repeated, lines continuously refined, and spaces mirrored and borrowed from a personal bank of memories and precious commissions.

'Consistency' is perhaps the life and death of this highly recognisable style. On the one hand it generously offers itself for consumption: it is enticing, elating, bold, uncompromising and pleasurable to experience. On the other hand, it runs the risk of being systematised which will ultimately result in it becoming a parody of itself. I am probably asking questions of this particular approach to design which the architect cannot answer, simply because he has not embarked on a course of evolving experimentation through his work. Instead, the product speaks for itself, and this is its strength.

The shifting vanishing points, blurred horizon lines, and erased corners are all techniques born from the interior. This is more of a condition of being within than of using or inhabiting the space. The eye is given free reign to travel. At this level we are observing the interior more as a phenomenological installation, testing our ability to perceive space as itself and not as a vessel, as, for example, in the saturated colour fields of James Turrell where light is harnessed as a medium.

The translation from minimalist installation art to a functional interior is an awkward leap, albeit a brave one. It demands absolute dedication to detail and a ruthlessness aimed towards rejection rather than inclusion. For example, skirtings, door/window frames, and cornices are excluded – all devices to cover joins. To achieve the desired result is labour intensive, time consuming and very expensive; a sympathetic client is essential, an unsympathetic one could destroy the result overnight.

The origins of this architecture could be traced back to primitive carved space, but it would be more accurate to place it within the context of twentieth-century minimalism. From this position the work comes into focus, yet it also exposes itself to some problematic contradictions. There is a heavy reliance on stud work, plasterboard and plaster, so much so that the structure is in fact excessively clothed, although appearing to be naked.

The promise in the photographic image (and this work is extremely photogenic) is one of permanence and stability, but because of the fleeting nature of the retail and leisure industry the places really only last as long as the hunger. Permanent materials such as stone, marble or granite would be redundant in this comparatively temporary field, but the solidity and gravity that these materials would give to the space, along with the craftsmanship needed in keying and joining them together, is what the promise holds. Assuming that a new generation of projects emerges – and I am sure it will – we will be seeing a maturation in harmony with presence of materials. It therefore comes as no surprise that patrons of minimalism tend to be museums and galleries of modern art, and the Church. The breeding grounds rest firmly in the academies and small practices. The two are often spliced together, in order to practise the precarious aesthetic these practitioners teach.

Since 1990 no dramatic change has occurred in Kovac's aesthetic; the changes that have taken place have been subtle, evidenced by a sophistication of finishes, details and a growing team of model makers, computer specialists, project managers and assistants. It is also of no surprise that in six years of producing a consistent body of work, a clear profile is developing which is exposing a deep maturity.

Professor John Andrews graduated from the Architectural Association, London, in 1977. He moved to Australia to become Head of the Department of Interior Architecture and Design at the Royal Melbourne Institute of Technology. He is Executive Editor of The Interior.

FROM ABOVE: Capitol, Melbourne, 1994; Urban Attitude, Sydney, 1996

Return of the Romantic

Peter King

At present Tom Kovac does not argue his architecture in tellings, diagetic descriptions,[1] narrations, or commentaries, but in showings: a mimetic[2] ensemble of images (sketches, plans, autocad wireframes and renderings, photographs) and actions (site alignments, specifications, materials schedules and prototypes, on-site improvisations and orders). (In 1964 Roland Barthes prophesied a 'linguistics of the signifiers of connotation, valid for articulated sound, image, gesture, etc'.[3] Inasmuch as this diagesis of mimesis, which would be a part of a 'psychologistic' project, has not yet distended, a dualism of the two fields remains operant in what Deleuze and Guattari term 'major' scales.[4])

In its formal and material manifestations, Kovac's argument aims at a *Darstellung*, a robust presentation of a fullness, a pleroma; and each manifestation – so the argument appears to run – has embedded within it a *mise en abyme* of another project sooner or later to swell the corpus: the repertoire is an index of repletion (repletion as either or both a beginning or an end). The self-reflection of the present work has stilled Kovac's practice of enchainment from design to design – noticeable anisochrony[5] and movement – in to a mirror, a dwindling sheen of idling and *gestus*. A mirror – here, geometrically sited, a series of optic functions, an analogy, not a trope – is the shelter of the proverbial 'emic' approach,[6] a holding pattern of the mimetic ensemble of the constituents of a system in terms of the position and function attributed in it by its users. (Here the emic approach would include the above mimetic ensemble, meetings with clients, the presentation, inhabitation and observation of the work.) Thus its reflection is self-reflection.

Und [...] kann auch [die romantische Poesie] am meisten zwischen dem Dargestellten und dem Darstellenden, frei von allem realen und idealen Interesse auf dem Flugel den poetischen Reflexion in der Mitte schweben, diese Reflexion immer wieder potenzieren und wie in einer endlosen Reihe von Spiegeln vervielfachen.[7]

(And Romantic poetry, free of all real and ideal concerns, is most of all capable of hovering on the wings of poetic reflection in the middle space between the presented and the presenting, magnifying this reflection again and again, multiplying it as in an eternal series of mirrors.)

An 'etic' approach[8] (external, taxonomic) identifies Kovac's present project as analogous to Friedrich von Schlegel's saturated Romanticism (Die Athenäums-Fragmente, 1798), in which the argument for a Romantic novel/poem is another Romantic novel/poem. For Schlegel, only an apparently etic 'divinatory criticism' is able to

dare characterise the ideal in Romanticism. Yet, as the above citation declares, the 'ideal' is excluded from, stated as in excess to, the wing-beaten middle. But the perturbed ether is also the void into which the excluded and excessive are introjected: criticism and the etic still obtain outside 'ecstatic', 'out of standing', but can only operate within:

In der romantischen Poesie sollte romantische Kritik mit der Poesie selbst verbunden sein.[9]

(In Romantic poetry, Romantic criticism ought to be united with poetry).

The criticism must be self-criticism, self-reflective. (On occasion this is agony, as is heard in Robert Klein's 1963 abjuration of his etic-close critical art: 'Sooner or later ... terms of reference have to be placed in the work itself.'[10] Here, for Klein, form and meaning, his subjects, have returned to the Romantic, become autists, indistinct, lost in shapes.) The forcible interpenetration of criticism and poetry would conjoin the emic with the etic in an anisochronic imbrication of discharges and implosions, a type of the linguistics – diagesis of mimesis – Barthes (as cited above) lassoed from an antiquity (Baif, Rousseau, Darwin) he anticipated. The synchronised or serial shocks – embraces, ejaculations – are not so reverberant in Kovac's work. He draws in. The critical reflection feeds inward and incites a centripetal construction that, in turn, grows inward; yet it is never impermeable. Its middle is perturbed by the enthymematic (intellectual discourse mimesis has rehearsed, a discourse that embeds fragments of diagesis in mimesis). Diagetic description, narrative and commentary (so long as the dualism of diagesis and mimesis holds) are not lacking in Kovac's project but are so immanent to it that the apparition of lack, neither discharge nor implosion, hovers in its voids and obscures its showings.

The emic approach demonstrated by Kovac wards off the excesses of psychologism, which tends to rely on diagesis in the act, the moments of momenta, of overcoding mimesis. But the project is also an injection of psychologism, a nonverbal symptom, (obscurely) showing (up) those Romantic excesses in a *Vorstellung*, a representation, in which that which is missing has to be inferred from the analogies (formal and material together, that is, a general impression) that produce the voids and obscurity. Gregory Bateson (1951) has suggested that in analogic 'models' (spaces, machines) 'changes in the external system can be represented by corresponding changes in the internal model'.[11] Kovac's emic spaces, 'internal models', withdraw from molar discourse into molecular happenings desiring 'to be something', as analogies loosed from, but also as, social or sociogenic impulses. The lack, that which is lost and that which seeks recompense in pleroma, observable (in a late Romantic glass) and performed in Kovac's work, is of social or sociogenic drives. Withdrawal, which has renounced chatter, tropes, programme, infrastructure, has valorised *Denkraum* (thinking space, intellectual distance) and also *Denkraumverlust* (the loss of them). Thus, Kovac's 'internal model', as argument, suffers, states and is not diminished by the injection of the outside which its swelling showing seems to prohibit. It is possible that that outside could be both the 'ideal' enchainment of the pleroma and its attenuation in 'real' space (the latter is the toll paid in casting off from the commonplace real). In Kovac's derealised spaces – in an excoriated contiguous metaphysics of light and planes – excluded architectonic materiality returns in monstrous bulk. Siegfried Kracauer (1922) has defined this return: 'Once in the "sphere of relaxation", however, [people] do not bring to bear the accumulated power of their spirit, but lapse into numbness, allowing heavy and slothful matter to gain power over them.'[12] Paradoxically, in Kovac's work the lack is of matter and the cry is for it. The project proceeds at present in ways analogous to those of the opera productions of Wieland Wagner at the 'New Bayreuth' (1951-67): a repertoire of hidden and hiding geometries and optics shoring up or down a Romantic abyss. What has been thought to have been seen as full is represented as a general impression induced by a stare at a skeleton. The immanence of *architecture parlante* is here an effect of the modernist mirror swallowing what it has seen.

Peter King is Co-ordinator of History and Theory in the Department of Interior Design, Faculty of the Constructed Environment, Royal Melbourne Institute of Technology.

Notes

1 'Pertaining to, or part of a given diagesis (*diagèse*) and more particularly, that diagesis [*telling*, recounting, as opposed to *showing*] represented by the (*primary*) *narrative*. Narratives, narrators and narratees, are characterizable in diagetic terms'. Gerald Prince, *A Dictionary of Narratology*, University of Nabraska Press (Lincoln and London), 1989, p20.

2 '... *Showing*, enacting (as opposed to *telling*, recounting)', ibid., p52.

3 Roland Barthes, 'Rhetoric of the Image', in *Image – Music – Text*, trans. Stephen Heath, Fontana (London), 1977, p50.

4 Gilles Deleuze and Félix Guattari, *A Thousand Plateaus*, trans. Brian Massumi, University of Minnesota Press (Minneapolis), 1987, pp75-110.

5 'A variation in narrative *speed*; an acceleration or a slowdown in tempo. The change from *scene* to *summary* or summary to scene constitutes an anisochrony'. Prince, *A Dictionary of Narratology*, p6.

6 'An internal and functional (as opposed to etic and taxonomic) approach to the study of (human) situations and productions. The emic approach defines and describes the constituents of a system in terms of the position and function attributed to them by its users', ibid., p25.

7 Friedrich Schlegel, 'Die Athenäums-Fragmente', in *Charakteristiken und Kritiken I*, Hans Eichner (ed.), Thomas-Verlag (Zurich), 1967, pp182-83.

8 'Rather than defining and describing the constitution from the point of view of one familiar with it, the etic approach uses criteria not intrinsic to the system to do it', Prince, *A Dictionary of Narratology*, p28.

9 Schlegel, 'Die Athenäums-Fragmente'.

10 Robert Klein, *Form and Meaning*, trans. Madeleine Jay and Leon Wieseltier, Viking (New York), 1979, p186.

11 Gregory Bateson, 'Information and Codification: A Philosophical Approach' in *Science and Literature: New Lenses for Criticism*, Edward M Jennings (ed.), Doubleday (Garden City, New York), 1970, p32.

12 Siegfried Kracauer, *The Mass Ornament: Weimar Essays*, trans. Thomas Y Levin (ed.), Harvard University Press (Cambridge, Mass. and London), 1995, p158.

Strike the Pose

Aaron Betsky

Tom Kovac creates work that seems to have emerged out of nowhere. It is particular to one place, but alien from it. It reminds one of work elsewhere in time and space, but has its own distinct appearance. Erupting out of the rather staid grid of Melbourne, one of those towns the English imposed on a landscape alien to the forms they used for their ordering systems, it screams with style and radical difference from everything around it. White, curved and rounded, it surrounds you, threatening to suffocate you with its surfeit of form. This is architecture that strikes a pose. It is both unfamiliar and strangely, sensuously, like some half-remembered embrace. It brings the body back into the city, but only as a skin, only as a gesture, only as a moment.

Such an attitude of architecture as gesture does not come out of an imagined 'noplace' or nowhere. It can only define itself in relationship to a particular order, to which it stands in contrast. It must also possess an inner logic, and there is an order here. It comes from the columns, in most cases. Streamlined, teardrop shaped and mushrooming they might be, but they do indicate a rhythm that, though it may no longer refer directly to structure, still ties down the enclosing shells. Those fragments of covering are the second order, one of curves that move always inward, scalloping around the inhabitant to hide the stretches. Behind these gestures, there are the walls themselves, curving away and onward, sweeping space with them as they go along. Windows, skylights and doors pierce these shells, as if indicating that there is a use to these spaces, not just a mood. Out of these layers of indication and envelopment, symmetries emerge. They are always local and often found by the architect on the site, when those forms curve towards each other and he ties them down, anchoring the composition with a sense that to every action there is an answering swoop or swerve.

So is it all style, with its own rules and its own context, but without recourse to a theory of endurance, logic and utopian pretension? Yes, it is an order of ornament that has become spatial. In these spaces, such traditional notions as type, functionality, structure or some notion of message matter little. It is all a gesture that envelops one, like a piece of clothing draped not over the body, but inside the body of a building, or instead of it. So these buildings do fit themselves in a particular tradition: that of the notion of architecture as a texture, a tent, or a tentative appropriation of spaces carved out from a world treated as either indifferent or inimical. The wall is not built, but draped, and the point is not to create a world that has a logic to teach us or a structure that both pre- and post-dates us, but to give us something to delight us, a pose.

These are buildings that are posed, draped and designed on the site. Computers help, as does a daily dose of supervision of the craftspeople building these elaborate constructs. Thus the architect is a dresser, working with a space as if it were a beautiful model or an actor full of effect. This does not mean that it is great architecture or 'just' fashion, but it is something more akin to what one would see in the fashion world than in the tradition of grand architecture.

So how does one judge this work? Certainly its logic derives to a large degree from its programmes, which up until now have been for retail stores, restaurants, clubs and private homes. These are not institutional situations. They demand something that above all seduces and offers an alternative. The outsider must be brought into the space, where she or he must be convinced to buy something, must find a convivial atmosphere, or must find the softness that our culture constructs as the home in contrast to the world of rules and regulations outside. Thus the building must become sexy or a container for a stand-in for sex.

This does not mean that this work stands in isolation, defined only by a designer as a specific response to a programme. This is work by Tom Kovac, working in Melbourne, Australia. Born in the former Yugoslavia, Kovac was trained at one of the world's most innovative architecture schools, the Royal Melbourne Institute of Technology (RMIT). The school has become a hotbed for expressionistic, deviant forms, ranging from the collages of Peter Corrigon to the computer models of its innovative students. Perhaps here Kovac learned how to make forms that are modern in their abstraction with a wilful lack of relation to their context, exhibiting an exuberance and willingness to take chances that untrained observers still associate with places removed from the constant critical abrasion found in the self-proclaimed capitals of Western culture.

I can be more specific than that. There is a direct line from the RMIT to the Architectural Association, though the relationship was not so strong when Kovac was a student there. Certainly some of the sources for his work can be found at the London institution, in the sweeping consumerist narratives of Nigel Coates, the filmic exuberance of Zaha Hadid, and the general interest in architecture as both part of pop culture and a tool of expression for a highly personalised design activity. Like Carlos Zapata, Mehrdad Yazdani and Ben van Berkel, to mention just a few widely separated designers, Kovac's work has been made possible, whether he likes it or not, by Hadid and Coates, and by the deconstruction of post-modernism into something that is no longer a language of works, but of built gestures.

Kovac's very position as an architect who is neither functionalist, rationalist nor concerned with the purveying of linguistic programmes already marks him as a member of the tribe of post-structuralists, 'deconettes' or 'later modernists' (depending on the definition most in favour). It also brings him closer to the continuum of ephemeral strategies of intervention that align architecture with other forms of projected culture. In the global architectural economy that has emerged in the 1990s, design is just one of many ways in which we inscribe our signature on the world of sprawl, and the better architects, such as Kovac, do this with style, grace and a self-conscious lack of pretension.

Within this family of forms, there is a serious movement, though its practitioners are such individualists that they would refuse to be lumped together. The 'new expressionism', to give it a shorthand designator, is one way of making buildings that depend on computers to make impossible shapes, and on a culture defined by fluid image chains to justify itself as the appropriate monumentalisation of such a world of collaged and morphed uncertainty. It seeks to fix the flows of capital into blobs that remain on the landscape. It challenges fashion, television and the internet at its own game. It is the closest that we have to an architecture that wants to look like a confirmation of the cultural conditions in which we live.

Certainly there are historical precedents for this work. They are the same ones that the designers once collectively called deconstructivist draw on in their thoroughly post-modern resurrection of the roots of modernism. Constructivism, which sought to create the uniforms to wear for a world in which even gravity would be defeated, and expressionism, which sought to draw its way out of the depressing realities of inter-war Europe, are clearly examples of similar work. The notion of architecture as defiant gesture that seeks to replace the realities of not just building types and social conventions, but the very physical relations between things, is at the heart of this tradition. In the latest version, however, history repeats itself, if not as farce, certainly as a pose. This is not Chernikov or Mendelsohn: this is a boutique in Melbourne.

Aaron Betsky is Curator of Art and Design at the San Francisco Museum of Modern Art. He has taught and lectured extensively, and is currently Adjunct Professor at the California College of Arts and Crafts. He is a contributing editor to many magazines, including Architecture, Blueprint *and* ID, *and has published eight books on architecture and design.*

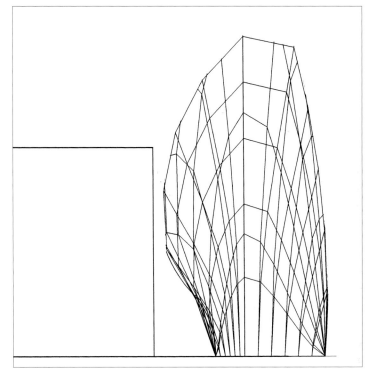

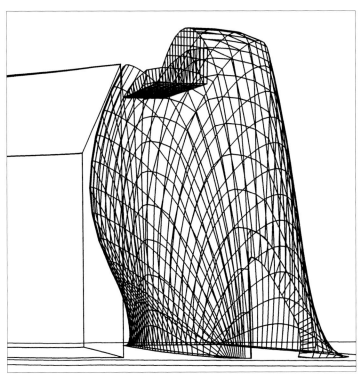

Barkly Apartments, Melbourne, 1996 – computer-generated net showing form inserted into the urban grid

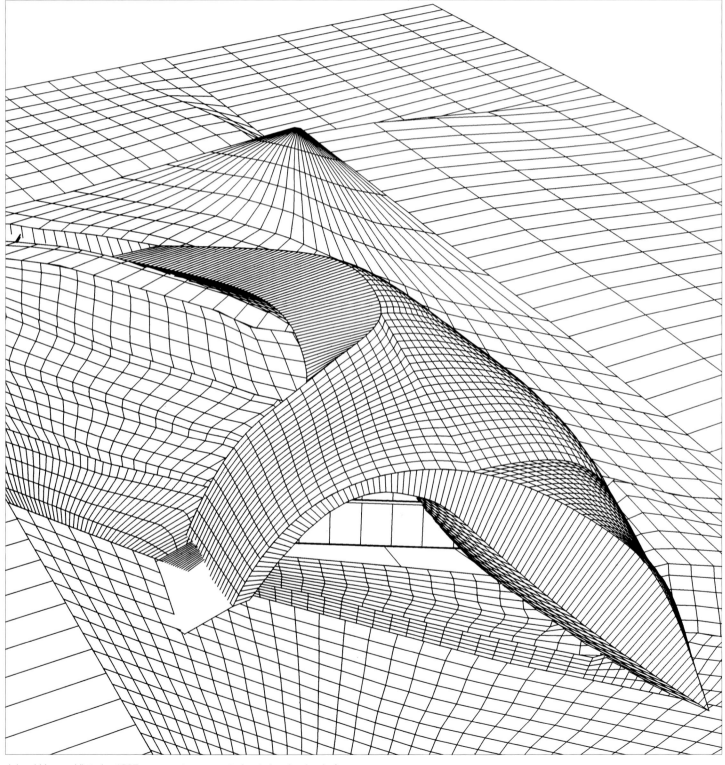

Island House, Victoria, 1997 – computer-generated net showing basic form

In a Field Condition

Georgi Stanishev

The Field is independent of materiality: it is not a state of matter but of space. (Albert Einstein, Special Theory of Relativity, 1905)

Since a piece of art or architecture is living on a crossroads of interpretations, any new reading should add to its vitality if it lays open yet another path to the poetic world of the author. The following survey aims to outline the possibility of understanding the architectural works of Tom Kovac as 'field-sensitive' devices. Within this interpretation the spatial formations designed by the architect are studied as manifestations of two different kinds of field – of energy and semantics – while Tom Kovac himself is placed in the position of a device that registers their vectors, compressions and expansions, and translates their physical or imaginative realms to the language of architectural forms and spaces.

The concept of the field is correlated to phenomena that occupy the zone of overlap between the material and the mental domains. The history of 'field-sensitivity' may be traced from the animistic, magical and mythological pictures of the world to present-day vitalism and the theory of morphic resonance. Fields considered as animated entities were related to place as the *genius loci*, or to time, as the *Zeitgeist*. The magnetic field was considered as an animated phenomenon until the seventeenth century, while the principle of gravitational attraction was, according to Voltaire, treated in France as equivalent to the physical attraction between human beings. The transition from object to field in recent theoretical and visual practice in art and architecture has its direct precedents in the twentieth-century avant-garde art. The abstract syntactic relations in the paintings of Vassily Kandinsky, the cloud-like concentrations of lines and dots in Piet Mondrian's works, and the overlapping vectors of energetic flows in the drawings of Paul Klee envisaged Einstein's sensation of physical space and presentimented the general shift from object to field conditions in art and in science. Today's hybridisation of art with digital technologies continues this tradition of understanding the field concept as an ambiguous entity belonging to both the physical and mental worlds, researched by the artistic and the scientific avant-garde alike. The architects working on the borderline between scientific and artistic domains are studying this area mostly with the means of high-tech computer equipment, using virtual modelling and operating with animation. Tom Kovac, however, is among the few individuals on the architectural horizon today whose contacts with the realm of the field conception seem to overcome the intermediation of technologies, and whose intuition substitutes the scientific speculation.

Learning the Field Sensitivity

Although Tom Kovac's *œuvre* covers a very short span of time, one may observe a certain evolution in his architectural work, from the static conditions of sculpted space towards a dynamic space charged by inner compressions and tensions. In the projects of the eighties and the early nineties the space has a referential power and is often read through the stagnant imagery of 'caves', 'wombs' or 'caverns'. The interior spaces coded by the *Gestalt* solid/void inversion either evoke metaphors of moulding the void as the carved mass of sculptural objects; trace organicist references to shells or worm holes; or are read through historicist parallels to the carved stone architecture of India, Tunisia or Helenistic Egypt.

It is difficult to perceive thresholds separating stages in Tom Kovac's practice, but his production of the last two years shows a new emancipation of matter. His latest projects seem to incorporate an expressive language which tells the story of their genesis, the rules of narration that govern the traces and diagrams indicating the invisible forces giving birth and embodied in the spatial structure of the architectural work itself. It seems also that, starting from approximately the mid-nineties, Tom Kovac's designs recognise another level of comprehension of space that acknowledges its field nature. This new vision of space leads to the neutralisation of the fundamental solid/void opposition and to the dissipation of their traditionally definite border. They become considered in terms of rates of compression of one and the same substance, similar to an isobar map representing fields of atmospheric pressure. This new direction of experimentation escapes historical or metaphorical referential frames and steps into the freedom of the field reality.

Field Energies

What reality? What types of energy are forming the field status of the architectural space in Tom Kovac's work? At least two of them may be scrutinised in more detail.

The first is related to the rituals of human movements in space: the rhythms of the repeated 'dance figures' of everyday life; the statistically most probable trajectories, crowded points and zones of relaxation, which form in space the distinction between the bulwarks of concentration and compression and the intervals of peace and dilution. Thus in the Succhi shop, the space lines are concentrated in the 'compression' points on both sides of the spatial tube and are disseminated on layers in the in-between zone, thus establishing different rates of consistency in the border surface. These differences follow almost diagrammatically the different concentrations of human movement in the space: tight and certain in the crowded points of entrances/exits, uncertain and dissolving in the expansion area. The 'layerisation' of the wall in the Urban Attitude project shows a similar intention to disseminate the solid border surface, to convert the transition from solid to void into a relativistic field. Human motions and behaviour as field-generating devices forming the architectural organism are clearly visible in Tom Kovac's sketches for the Capitol nightclub, where trajectories of movement construct the differentiation of the architectural space. Besides this pulsation, which reflects the compression/dissolution rhythm of human movements, there are types of motions that presuppose uniform, indifferent dynamics as the transition path passing through the whole building body, as in the Island House.

The other type of energy field ruling Kovac's architectural spaces belongs to the realm of gravitation, to geological forces and landscape relief vectors, kindred to wind and water flows and pressures. It appears as if Tom Kovac possesses a specific sense to register these formation fields, as well as the ability to translate and convert them into a system of architectural expression. Not all of these field forces are identifiable and exist physically. The important point is that they exist in Tom Kovac's poetic world; the results of their actions, the directions and strength of their energy are made readable through the formal and spatial structures of his projects. Thus, in the architect's most recent works a strong visionary motif that resembles a rooted wing often appears in a double role – both as a basic configuration of the work and as a sensitive device, a resonator able to register the field forces and compressions of the site. It is bent to the slope of the site in the Island House; twisted, screwed and grooved in the Pontian Centre; and is simply cut through by a section in the Pless House project. The resulting configurations of this spatial 'icon' seem to be generated by some unknown powers that subordinate the matter and space in the same natural way that iron filings are made to follow the magnetic field lines: in both cases the spatial structure reflects the most 'economic' form in given field conditions. This process of reflection is similar to the way an aeroplane wing is designed to withstand the aerodynamic stresses of air pressure. It shows a type of economy and energetic suitability that makes the conceptual bridge between Tom Kovac's work and minimalism an ethic doctrine.

Although both types of these energy fields work in Tom Kovac's compositions in a symbiotic complementation and interaction, they result in two genetically and topologically different types of space. While the compression/decompression fields of human activities generate spatial bubbles, canals or paths that are blown inside the solid mass of his buildings, the powers of the gravitational field fold, bend and twist the building mass to cover, fence, border and enclose a section of the outer space, thus converting it into a semi-interior one. The interplay of both spatial genotypes in the latest of Kovac's works gives a topological freedom that allows architectural elements to be solid and void simultaneously, depending on what level of the structure we consider them. Thus, both types of spaces are clearly articulated in the Island House; here the rooted wing is both a massive vault in relation to the living area and an emptied solid – continuing the series of inner-room spaces – grown as a bubble inside and possessing its own walls. Continued, this topology will inevitably lead us to the sequence similar to the hierarchy of fractal morphology.

Architectural Links

The originality of Kovac's expressive system presupposes that it would be more useful to find historic support for his work by outlining precedents of a 'field-type' of architectural behaviour, rather than tracing direct parallels with concrete works.

One such precedent can be identified in Rudolf Steiner's architectural experimentation. In these works Steiner constructed a set of spatial reactions to the movements of invisible forces which act by inflating the volumes of the spaces, by leaving traces and grooves when trespassing through the building volume.

Another precedent can be found in the works and texts of Louis Kahn, even though Kovac's expressive means are a long way from Kahn's. The common denominator linking their poetics lies in the principle of mass-to-space inversion, which in Kahn's work rises to the level of a basic poetic metaphor. The Kahnian space has the ability to grow inside massive elements as columns and walls, gradually converting solids into hollowed spatial shells, similar to the bubble spaces in Tom Kovac's houses that grow inside the solid wall and roof elements.

Another correlation which may generate a context for Kovac's works can be traced to the poetics of Alvaro Siza. His sensory architecture is similarly correlated to flows of matter and energy registered on the place, converting the architectural work into a spatial knot that ties the composition not only to the site but also to spatial vectors and universal co-ordinates.

It is clear that Kovac's multivalent architecture affords reading at radically different levels. On a phenomenological level, the architectural poetics of Tom Kovac are close to Kahn's metaphysical conversions of the dark mass into a lightened void. In relation to energetic and dynamic reactions, his blown spaces and bent surfaces are rooted in a soil shared with Steiner's 'imprints of forces', while the abstract sensitivity of his works to the universal vectors is most comparable to that of Siza.

Poetics of Resonance

These correlations to the poetic strategies of selected architects do not, however, cover the more important question: what is the general type of artistic consciousness to which Kovac's poetics belong?

Sensitivity to the natural world and its energies places the works of Tom Kovac within the Romantic tradition. In the most general sense, this is a vision of the poet/architect as an individual who is able to establish an intuitive correlation between the world and his own mental universe, and to express their resonance in his art. Thus, the literature of nineteenth-century European Romanticism operated with Nature as with an esoteric language, with the poet considered as the sensitive instrument whose mission it was to find the keys to transmit these messages through his art.

But do these fields, converted by Tom Kovac's imagination into a powerful architectural expression, obtain an identifiable physical nature? As long as it is not possible to distinguish truth from poetic vision within a piece of art, the differentiation between the real and the imaginative forces in Kovac's works is, in fact, not a relevant task. In a similar manner, just as the shape of mountains allows a reading of the geological forces that created them, so the buildings of Tom Kovac give us the possibility of unveiling the energetic fields as the immanent part of a poetic reality made accessible and tangible through his works. Within the Romantic vision, Nature is taken as an expressive vehicle for the spiritual state of the poet. No reader of Lermontov is interested in whether the rocks and mountain peaks, the stormy squalls and thunders belong to the physical world since they are read as diagrams and traces of the poet's own emotional condition.

Within the poetic domain of an artwork the dualisms of truth and illusion, matter and mind are resolved by the universality of the field conception, equally present in the physical realm of the gravitation and the mental realm of the semantic field. Thus what Kovac's architecture stands for is his own poetic world, and what is registered by the architect's spatial intuition and resonance are the storms and hurricanes that take place in it.

Georgi Stanishev is an architectural critic and editor of the 'Concept' feature in World Architecture *magazine. He teaches architectural theory at the University of Architecture and Building, Sofia, Bulgaria.*

Island House, Victoria, 1997 – computer-generated drawing showing skeletal composition

Atlas House, Melbourne, 1996 – under construction

Neither Carved nor Moulded

An Architecture of the Third Term

Leon van Schaik

Building material is the medium of architecture ... can there be any other? Yes ... instead of letting his (sic) imagination work with structural forms, with the solids of a building, the architect can work with the empty space – the cavity – between the solids and consider forming the space as the real meaning of architecture.

Thus Rasmussen defines the ancient duality in *Experiencing Architecture*.[1] The information age has architects adding a third term to this canon: the surface. As techno-nomads we float above the ground surveying the terrain through surveillance screens: windscreens, computer screens, TV screens. The hard-won tactility of architectural reality fades into an undifferentiated array of surface effects all conveyed with the comfort of air conditioning and piped music. An architecture of expression has emerged, competing in its coding with film. I want to demonstrate that, in contrast, Kovac is making an architecture out of this third term, and that he is doing so by engaging us in conflicting expectations, that his work is concerned primarily with the poles of the duality. I want to argue that it is precisely by making it impossible for us to incorporate either into our mental space that we come to fully experience a spatiality of the present rather than the caverns or objects of the past.

At first sight Kovac appears to be fighting a rear-guard battle against this emerging world. His office is strewn with sketches that explore and re-explore cave-like, womb-like forms that fold and twist over sites, ingesting and distributing light across their complex moulded walls. Rough models are made and scanned into computers by technicians, who, hunched over the sketches, transform them into measurable and constructible data. To visit a completed project is to be swept away in flowing lines of light; space made somehow palpable by the stretched enfolding surfaces. We can imagine the teams of artisans dressed in white applying the thick gesso to the armature of the drawings, trowelling and smoothing, adding white and grinding until the space is released in strict accordance with those drawings.

This archaic vision is in accord with Tom's citation of Barbara Hepworth's sculpture as a resonant practice. He writes that he finds the 'formal power' and 'fluidity' of her work creates a 'transparency' because the 'mass excludes and at once retains a mystique alluding to an invisible spatial component'. This gives us a clue to how he has imagined his architecture of the third term. Fantasies of sculptural crafting misread his interest and mislead us as to the essential purpose of the multitudes of drawings that he produces, rendering them as couturier doodles that skilled workers will then bring into being. These volumetric caves are in fact made from standard flat sheets of gypsum board bent over framing. The drawings find ways in which to pull curves through junctions between the boards, such that the illusion of continuous sculptured form is maintained. There are situations that can only be worked through on site, but there you will find only the architect, his assistant and a jobbing carpenter or two, as they wet and bend a board into shape.

Having seen Tom's early success – the Succhi shoe shop in Swanston Walk – ripped out recently, I suppose that we have to take a commercially contingent ephemerality for granted. But how can this ephemerality be related to the sculptural eternity that Hepworth, Serra and Judd imply in their work? Kovac's appearance on the British scene at the RIBA exhibition *Architecture on the Horizon* (1996) has made me wonder what this work looks like to European eyes. Up until now I have been prepared to take Tom's sculptural references at face value, laughing with him as he quips that 'architecture is sculpture with plumbing'. Under the influence of this coding, I have referred to Kiesler's work as a possible precedent. Now I wonder how that modernist's sense of material purity and geometrical integrity can be congruent with Kovac's surfaces. This despite the fact that there is a compelling sense that the interior of the Ryan Warehouse has eventuated through thrusting some wonderfully carved elements down into the orthogonal carcass of the existing building; and despite the fact that the Island House proves that Tom Kovac's vision is not only internal, that he has the extraordinary capacity to generate convincing taut organic form in both the positive and the negative.

In Kovac's case it makes some sense to claim kinship with the effects that these sculptors have caused when one considers that in the main we Antipodeans are aware of this work through photographs alone. We thus read volumes and solids as surfaces not as the carved or modelled matter evident to the first-hand witness. We turn light and shadow into substance by seeking to emulate the photographs. But how do eyes tutored by seeing, and hands tutored by caressing Barbara Hepworth's sculptures at first hand, read Kovac's architecture? Do they see in the photographs the carved solids that they have grown up alongside? I suspect that they do.

Is this paradoxical mutual misreading consequential? After all, we southerners have been misreading the world through flat images for a long time – a northern inversion is ironically apt. What will they make of it, these enthralled critics, when it is revealed to them that this work occupies the zone between solid and cavity? That this is neither carved nor moulded form?

Atlas House, Melbourne, 1996 – under construction

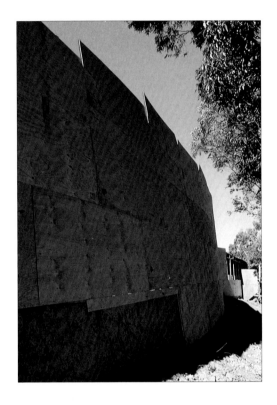

Will they understand that in our new world, surface experience is dominant? Migrants denied access to the micro-histories of their new country see everything as surface, as Paul Carter has explained in *Living in a New Country*.[2] To appreciate this the non-migrant would have to conceive of their favourite sculptures flattened into momentary images, fleetingly glimpsed in books, without scale – timeless, elusive. All the matter emptied away. The thought of Hepworth hollowed out! It is for these reasons that I have written that Kovac seeks to reveal the new in the new world, and sets himself in contradistinction to the imported legal frameworks that define modern Australian space.

The very 'inauthenticity' of the construction is that which gives the work its edge. The framing that we do not see, unless invited by the architect to look through a trap door, sets in space the series of points needed to hold and bend and tie the surface into place. These spurs and spars and half trusses and beams quite literally register the architect's conception in space. To invert the inversion, I claim that we have seen this inauthenticity before: in that wonderful space between the external and the internal domes of Sir Christopher Wren's St Paul's.

The space that is generated in Kovac's work puts me in mind of Homer Fardjadi and Mohsen Mostafadi's term 'delayed space'. We have to find ways of describing the slow turgidity of the space compressed into the rear of the Gan House, and the space that wells up at the opposite end. Slow space gives way to speedy space in the entry sequence of the Atlas House, before depositing you in the dappled space of the pool room. Being inside a sculpture is after all not simply a matter of making the piece big enough to walk under. Kovac has indeed visualised space that exists within mass, and the surface of that conception compresses and releases space in a new way.

In the early sixties Richard Hamilton, a key exponent of Pop Art, referred to a two-piece carving I had made in his class and had painted enamel blue and red as a 'Pop Hepworth'. The piece was a shocking image to sensibilities attuned to the natural (pure) properties of materials. Looking again, I could see that the paint hardened the surfaces and made them more object-like, less part of the 'natural' world of bones and pebbles. If I look to future possibilities in Kovac's work, I suppose that I look forward to more people being able to engage in the mischievous delights of the architect's peep show into what lies behind the skin. Also, I await with bated breath the emergence of colour on to those white, tight surfaces. Already, as in the Capitol nightclub, he uses light to wash colour into some spaces. Applied colour may heighten the

contemporary ambiguity of his work, which, as I have tried to argue, alternates between solid and cavity just as the eye fashions a neon edge from opposing colours. Kovac's surfaces shimmer in the edge between the two familiar means of making architecture, and are best conceived of as inhabiting that new zone, even though in some lights and at some times of day they exude the brooding mass of the solids that they have invaded (see the Pontian Centre). One day perhaps a surface will absorb light more deeply – like Yves Klein's *International Blue* – and another play in the surface will begin. But for now Kovac insists that pure light and white are enough of a game, and indeed there is much still to be explored in that regard. And with such delight at hand, we can afford to wait.

Notes

1 Rasmussen, *Experiencing Architecture*, Chapman and Hall (London), 1964.

2 Paul Carter, *Living in a New Country*, Faber and Faber (London), 1992.

Succhi, Melbourne, 1991 – skin and armature

Projects
1990-97

I was born in Celje, Slovenia, as were my parents, I arrived in Melbourne, Australia, at the age of ten. I speak Slovenian with my family as I have always done, while speaking English with the English, Italian with the Italians and French with the French.

My formative years inevitably shaped my ideals and my memory. I grew up in a land described in fairy tales – a castle on the hill, swords and Celtic hats buried just beneath the soil from days gone by, The landscape was dense, writhing and rich, a far cry from the openness that bewildered me on my arrival in Australia. But they are the obvious things.

I remember the hearth of the home and sitting on top of it to keep warm. My house, at the edge of the city, was old and heavy and thick with incredible views and forests to play in. My affinity with the ski slopes and cutting through the snow, even as a young boy, instilled a sense of freedom and control into me, the ease of intuitive navigation through the runs has not left me.

It has always been an education and inspiration to visit members of my family or friends who live elsewhere. The fundamental common conditions of all cultures help to invigorate faith in humanity and reinstate global connections. Being privy to cross-cultural experiences has helped me believe that anything is possible.

Architecture is an obsession. I labour until the building is working, functionally, formally and conceptually – I believe that it is possible to obtain all three together. I prefer to investigate beyond conventional building and material means to produce work that does not deny the original intention. Without pioneers no new ground can be fostered.

My work is a homogenous entity driven by its site and context. It does not aim at telling a narrative, it aims at hitting the button inside everybody who can respond to its ability to just be. I'm not straining to invent an identity for Australian architecture and perhaps that may explain the serenity of my work as opposed to a loaded, contorted, confused architecture. Eventually through its own proliferation, it will just become Australian architecture.

Tom Kovac

Melbourne
Squire Boutique
1990

The Squire Boutique was sited in a commercial development in South Yarra, a fashionable retail area in Melbourne. Comprising a shop and a separate space for wholesale operations, it was the first project by Tom Kovac to be built. (It was demolished in 1994 when the clothes shop closed down.)

The design focused on optimising the relationship between the street and interior, a balance of detail and atmosphere. The scheme was contained within a defined rectilinear volume offset from the front entrance by a high ceiling and wall that extended the length of the space. A central dividing wall articulated the two primary spaces: the retail and wholesale areas. Various utility openings developed the connection to the offices and storage space at the rear of the shop. The ceiling peeled away from the side walls and dropped very low, intensifying the transition between the public and private aspects of the space. The plan, volume and ceiling forms resulted from this strategy of accommodating the functional aspects of the brief. The depth of field was accentuated by the deep ceiling which defines the space and heightens the experience of the interior. Kovac's intervention in this building was limited to the ceiling and walls due to a restricted budget, which also confined the choice of material to plaster sheeting.

Melbourne
The Cherry Tree
1990

The Cherry Tree is an existing pub located in an industrial area of Melbourne, on a site bounded by a sweeping arterial road and a railway overpass. Kovac's main objective in remodelling the building was to unify the interior into a single space, articulated by the existing walls and structure. Within this the client specified three distinct areas: the front room facing the street was to become a bar; the back room, a restaurant and performance space; and level one, the offices and management zone. The external form of the building had to be retained due to the local authority's heritage requirements. However, the interior did call for a remodelling of the site's irregular shape, though the original building's central core had to be retained as it contains the services around which the spaces are organised.

Accepting the operating conditions, the entire ground floor was divided by the services and the rear extended by 100 square metres to open the pub into a large space which also accommodated the mandatory off-street parking and storage facilities. The entire ground floor hinges on a narrow circulation passage; this is the ordering device for the distribution of the formal mass and it's spatial 'scraping' within the shell of the building. The front entrance engages a floating ceiling which continues over the bar and the plaster-encased stair to engage the void above, vaulting to the rear and up to an ovoid cupola light source. The plaster form is supported by the existing walls and ceilings, which guide the sculpture from a ceiling level of 2.4 metres to a height of 6 metres. It is intended as a three-dimensional form shaping the interior and engaging the exterior. The continuity of space ruled out the use of beams or columns. Instead, transitions are made through sculptural shapes and a limited use of colour, which emphasise form through contrast.

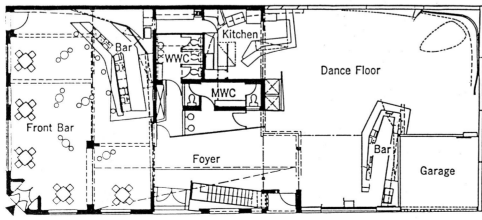

Ground floor plan

FROM ABOVE: Ceiling detail; view from entrance of main bar

FROM ABOVE: Restaurant skylight detail; view of kitchen servery

Melbourne
Succhi
1991

Created within the shell of a Victorian building, the Succhi shoe shop injected an architectural form and presence into the ephemeral commercial arena of retail interiors. Succhi was sculpted on site by issuing daily instructions, based on initial sketches, while building at full scale; thus the different symmetries and lines were edited in a way which would have been impossible to control from the drawing board.

The plaster-lined forms of the ceiling and wall merged, forming a continuous spatial sequence that extended over the existing rectilinear space. The internal skin pushed out to engage the street facade, visually connecting to the outside fabric; its invisible plaster thickness articulating a formal dialogue between existing and inserted form. The austere interior was produced as a coherent extruded space that exuded a sense of permanence and

stood in contrast to the ordered street-scape outside. The space was conceived around two principal elements – the new facade and the inner void – which were interrelated to imply a scale and form to legitimise the building's existence beyond its commercial reality. (When the shoe shop closed down in 1996 Kovac's work was demolished; all that now remains is the door handle.)

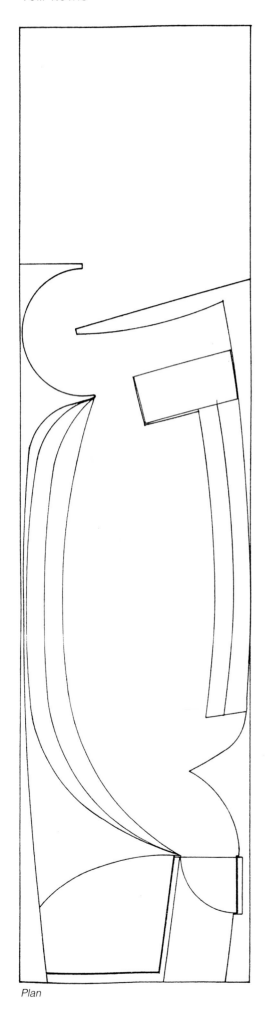

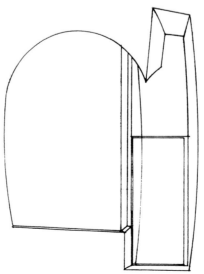

Plan

Front elevation

Melbourne
Gan House
1993

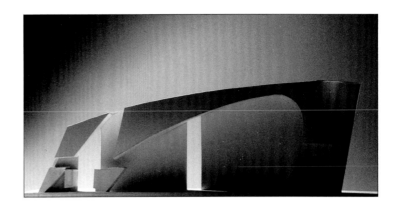

Kovac's brief was to create a living and dining area for an existing house in a 100-square-metre addition. His design is a bold response to a period house. The new building rejects a sympathetic or contextual response to its setting. Conceived as an autonomous entity, no effort is made to reconcile it to the fabric of the older structure, to which it is tentatively connected by a glazed transparent spine.

The co-existence of the two structures brings into question preconceptions about traditional and conventional inhabitation

and spatiality. The new addition generates its own presence and mysterious spatial volume. The form is generated as a single volume over 5 metres high, with continuous curved walls and vertical slit openings for windows and entry points. Around the main pavilion are clustered smaller ancillary spaces for laundry, bathroom, and entrance and storage areas. The new building is placed at the rear of the site, independent from the boundaries and the original house.

The construction technique used responded to Kovac's desire to create a

building that could be read as a monolithic form against the fragmented urban condition. It also called into question existing planning codes and the restrictions they exert upon architectural expression. By gradually sloping the canted timber walls, Kovac achieved the necessary building setbacks. These walls were lined with structural wire mesh and plywood sheets, which were in turn coated with a fine stucco rendered finish. This gave the building the articulation and appearance of an independent and clear form.

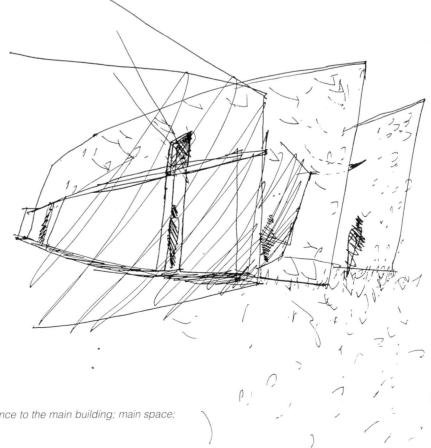

OPPOSITE: View through to the kitchen and entrance to the main building; main space;
ABOVE: Preliminary sketch

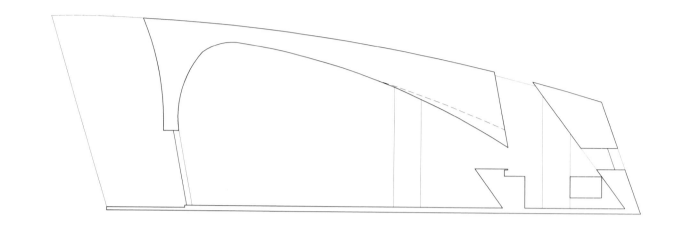

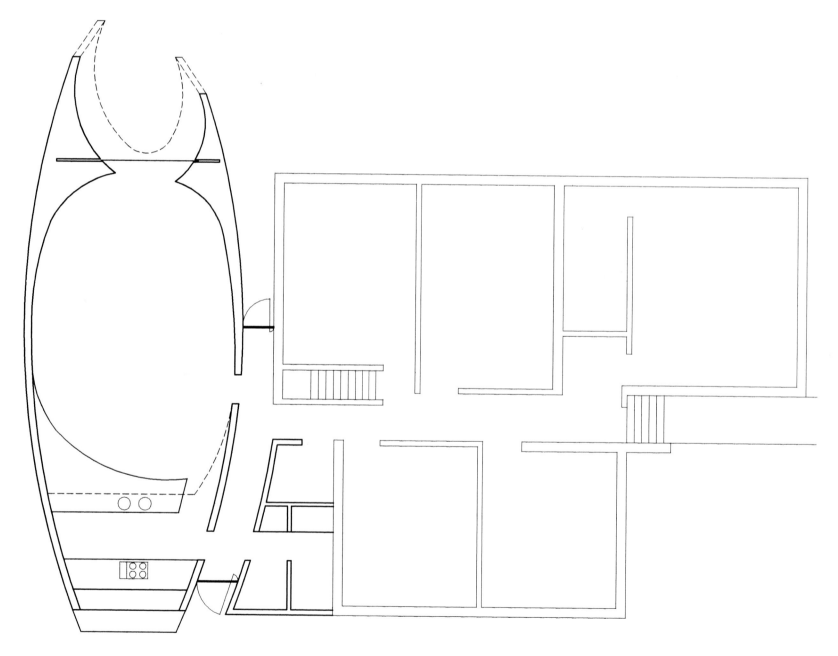

FROM ABOVE: Section; plan

Construction process

Melbourne
Capitol
1994

The Capitol nightclub is located in the basement of a commercial building. One of the programme's main criteria was to retain as much as possible of the existing structure, due to the loads of the building above. Kovac's scheme was also constrained by the three spaces available which varied in height. Within these tight parameters the brief required two separate bar zones and a central dance area. Working around the existing plant room, offices and fridges, Kovac's white stud and stucco interior skin discreetly wraps itself around the existing basement walls and columns, filling the shell with opacity and transparency of form. Spatial scraping of folded and buckled ceilings and cyke-type walls creates an illusion of horizontal depth. The horizontal also spreads underneath the compressed vertical dimension as the ceiling cranks down to a height of only 1.7 metres above the bars. Artificial light sources are recessed into this smooth, draped, lunar crust; slotted, cut or folded they appear to impregnate the form from another source. The carved white space is optically transformed through the movement and colour of computerised artificial light.

The plan and form are foetal-like, containing three pods that rotate around a central core which is pierced by three existing columns. The pods designate dance, sitting and drinking areas.

Sketch of interior

FROM ABOVE: Ceiling detail; main bar

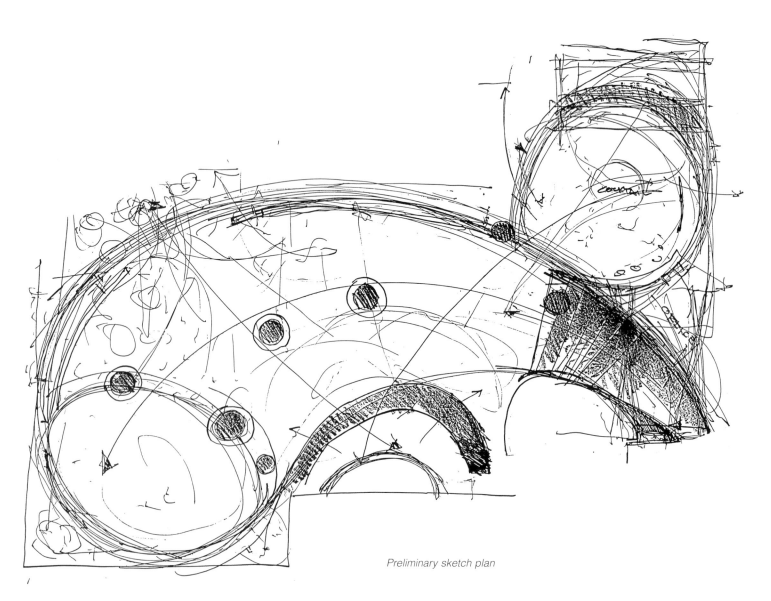

Preliminary sketch plan

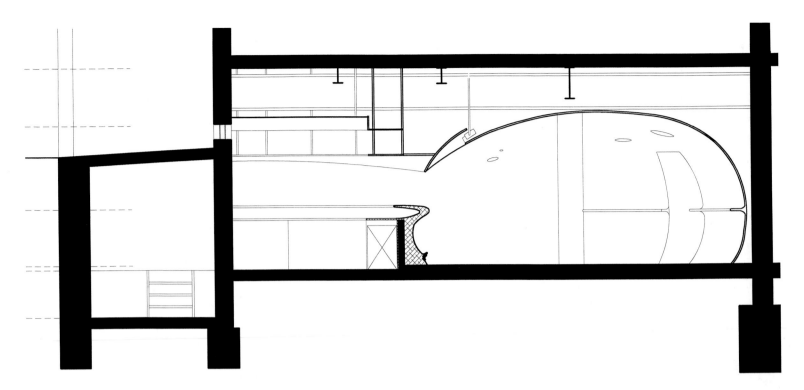

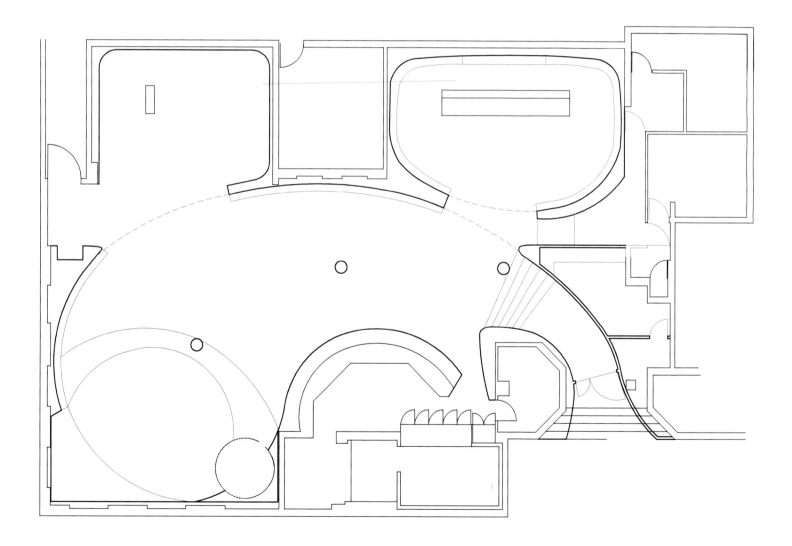

FROM ABOVE: Cross section; plan

Melbourne
Gibbs Church Conversion
1994

The task was to reconstruct the first-level section of a bluestone church, which had already been partially redeveloped. The client's main concern was that a sleeping area, a bathroom and a study should be provided. The small space is divided into two areas by an existing steel staircase, which emphasises the vertical nature of the building. This and the high portal ceiling at first suggested an isolated form within the space that could take advantage of and express this verticality. The initial model emphasised a formal insertion and a spatial connection between the existing church walls and the roof. The idea of constructing a form which engages the old with its own complexity and interwoven relationship was lessened in the final scheme (completed in 1995). The precise rectilinear form of the church made it possible to insert an autonomous object into the space and to legitimise the void.

The vertical nature of the space is emphasised by stretching the cylindrical form of the bathroom element through the ceiling. The placement of the bathroom pod off-centre creates a focal and discrete object in the room, creating a new counterpoint for the space without a formal division. The bathroom remains accessible from all areas.

Directly next to the cylinder is a linear white form which emphasises the horizontal aspect of the room. Its function as a wardrobe and storage unit is concealed, as are its openings at both ends of the wall.

These elements are signs of newness and intervention – a permeable vertical solid and a horizontal body set against the existing bluestone structure. Both define and modify the church, offering a redistribution of space.

OPPOSITE AND LEFT: Model shots of initial scheme

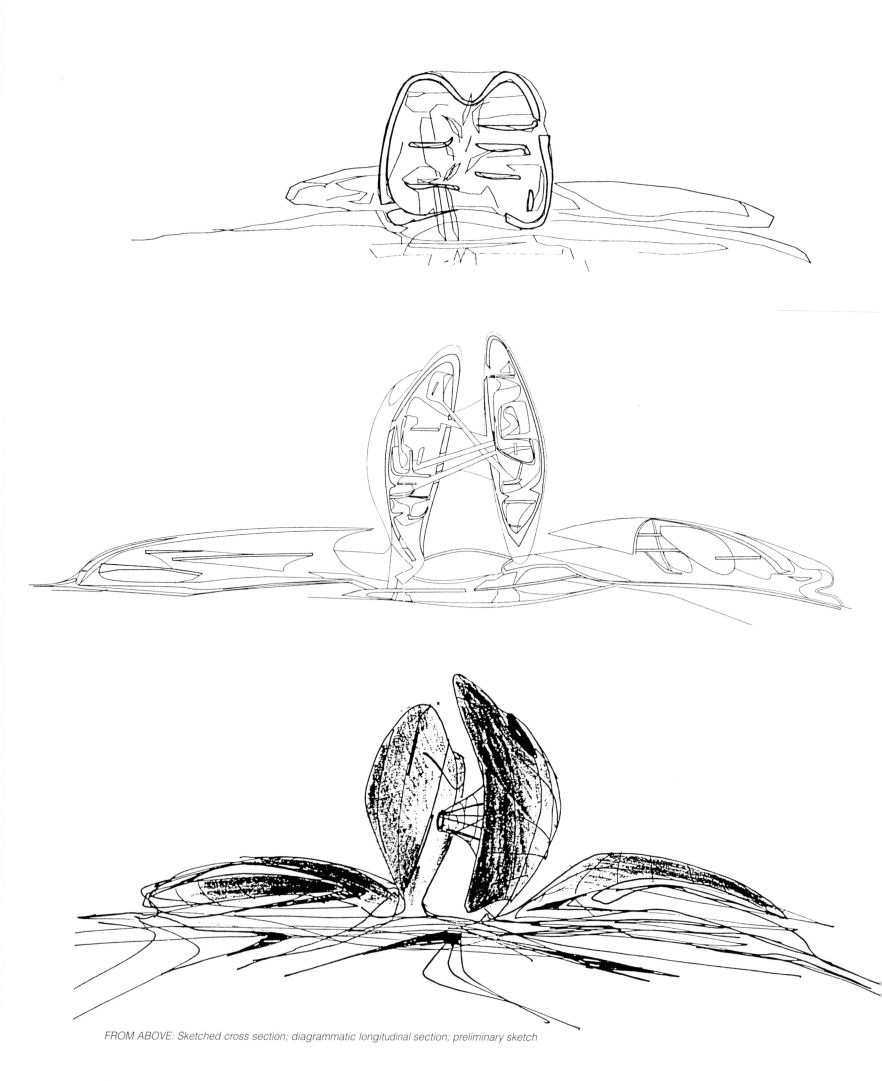

FROM ABOVE: Sketched cross section; diagrammatic longitudinal section; preliminary sketch

Melbourne
Museum of Victoria
1994

The brief for this scheme, which was produced as a competition entry, asked for a landmark building that would create a focus for the city on a site adjoining an exhibition building.

The classical proportions of the existing building and its central spire are echoed in the new twin towers. The proposal transforms these slender towers into vertical exhibition zones with escalators to enable movement between the different levels. The building's glass and aluminium forms transform from solid during the day to translucent at night.

The new spires draw in the city at ground level through underground access from the parkland, and connect to the existing building. At this level the museum rises to form a platform which provides circulation and a setting for public activities and commercial parts of the programme. Temporary exhibitions and events are housed on the first three floors, which are horizontal plates; these allow the parkland and natural light to filter through. Amenities and administration are retained at the lower levels which also have access to the outside gardens. The towers are transparent volumes containing vertical and horizontal interconnecting exhibition spaces; their internal forms suggest sculptural solids of different scales which provide a varied journey rather than a straightforward procession through the museum.

While Kovac had always envisaged a vertical development of the site, its location at the centre of a public garden made this a delicate issue. Therefore his solution proposes superimposing different layers of materiality that dissolve into the landscape. On the other hand, introducing a high building into this urban setting was a deliberate attempt to disassociate with the language of existing exhibition halls.

The aim was to create a building which would counter its scale with translucency and an opaqueness in which the reflection of the gardens could be seen. The facade was important in establishing the interior – an open-plan space adaptable to different possibilities and programmes.

Level 1 plan of towers and administration block

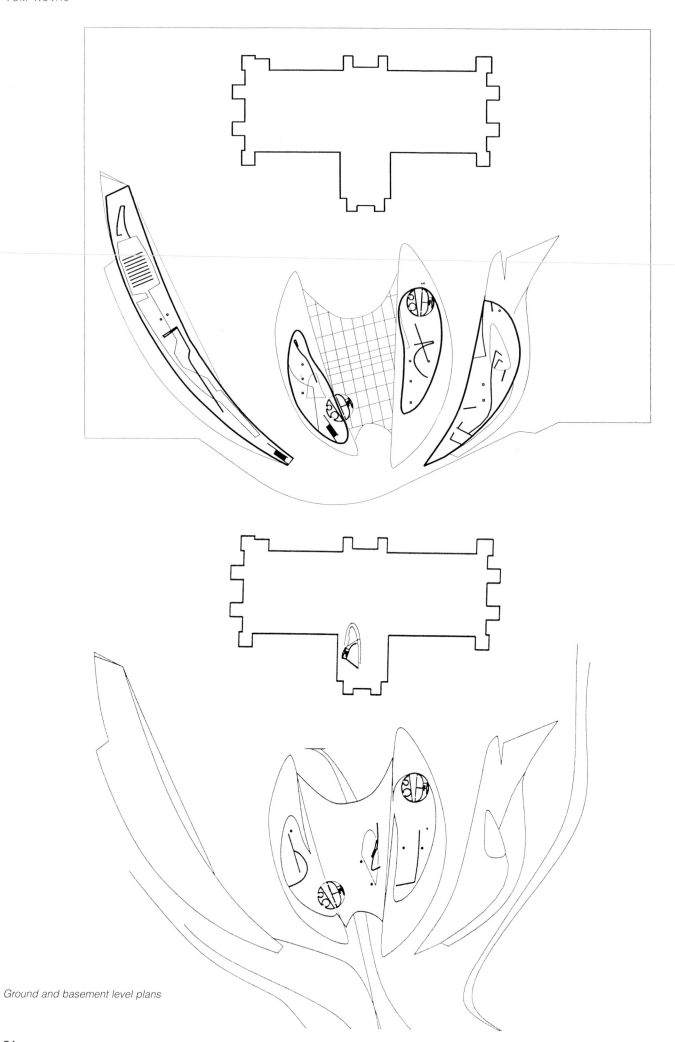

Ground and basement level plans

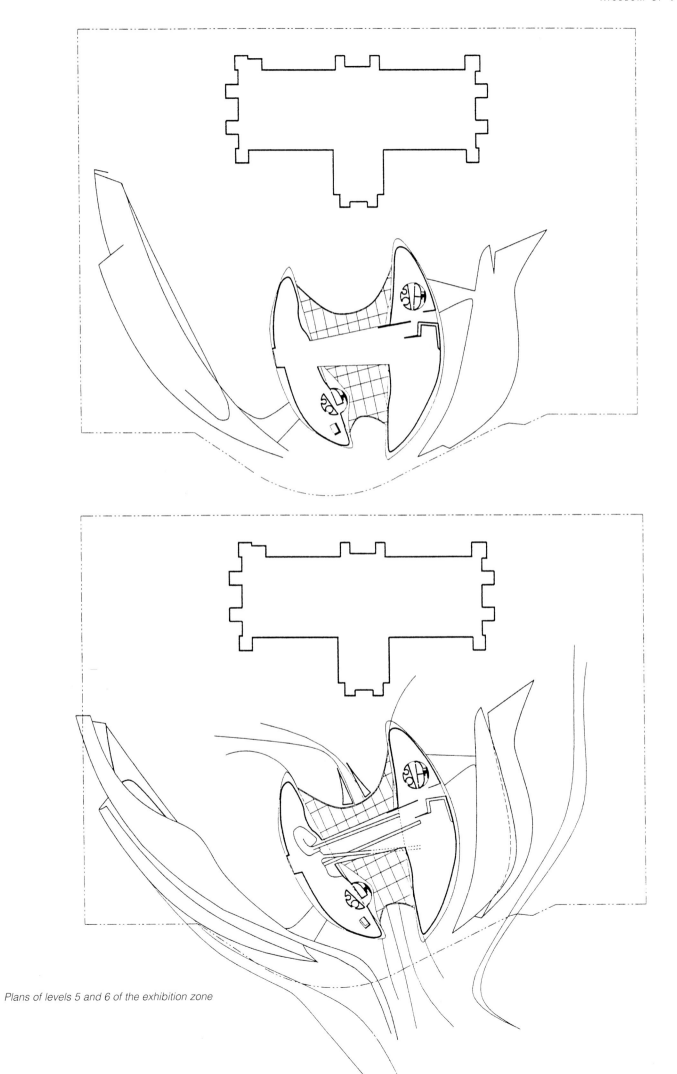

Plans of levels 5 and 6 of the exhibition zone

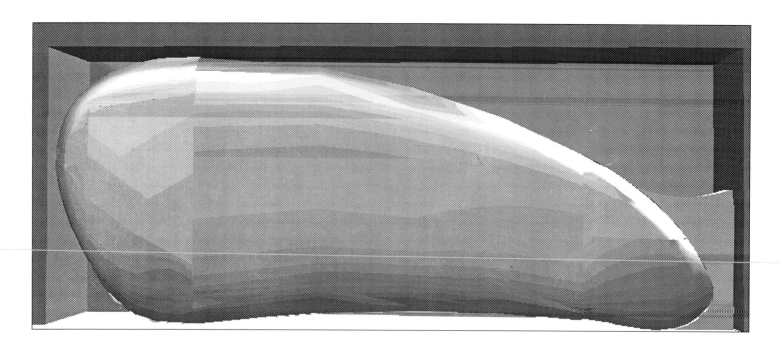

Melbourne
Curve Gallery
1995

This commission came from an important contemporary art gallery that required a space for exhibiting architecture. Kovac's initial project, illustrated here, establishes a centre for activity which uses the existing gallery as a foyer for visitors to the architecture space and vice versa for art openings. The final, built version of the scheme has lost some of the innovative spatial massing of this earlier version, as Kovac was asked to modify his project to a more conventional form. The new gallery is set in a vault formerly used for storage. The small proportions of this room – 2.4 × 4.0 × 5.0 metres – offered a jewel-like enclosure which could be intensified by the presence of an exhibition. The scheme removes the door of the existing vault, which connects it to the main gallery, while retaining its height and narrow opening. The intention was to create a seamless space without planes that would allude to an illusionary depth of field, an empty space in the built mass. The internal floor, walls and ceiling were to be white with curved edges, constructed from plaster sheets cut to shape and bent into form. The floor, covered by a fine rubber membrane of the type usually applied to tennis courts, was designed to merge with the wall. The ceiling vaults from the doorways to its maximum height and is lit by a system mounted in the carcass of its form. A projector facility was also to be housed in the ceiling for projection and sound installation. The space is conceived as a simple and minimal volume.

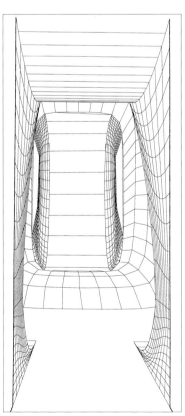

OPPOSITE AND ABOVE: Initial scheme, computer-generated models and net

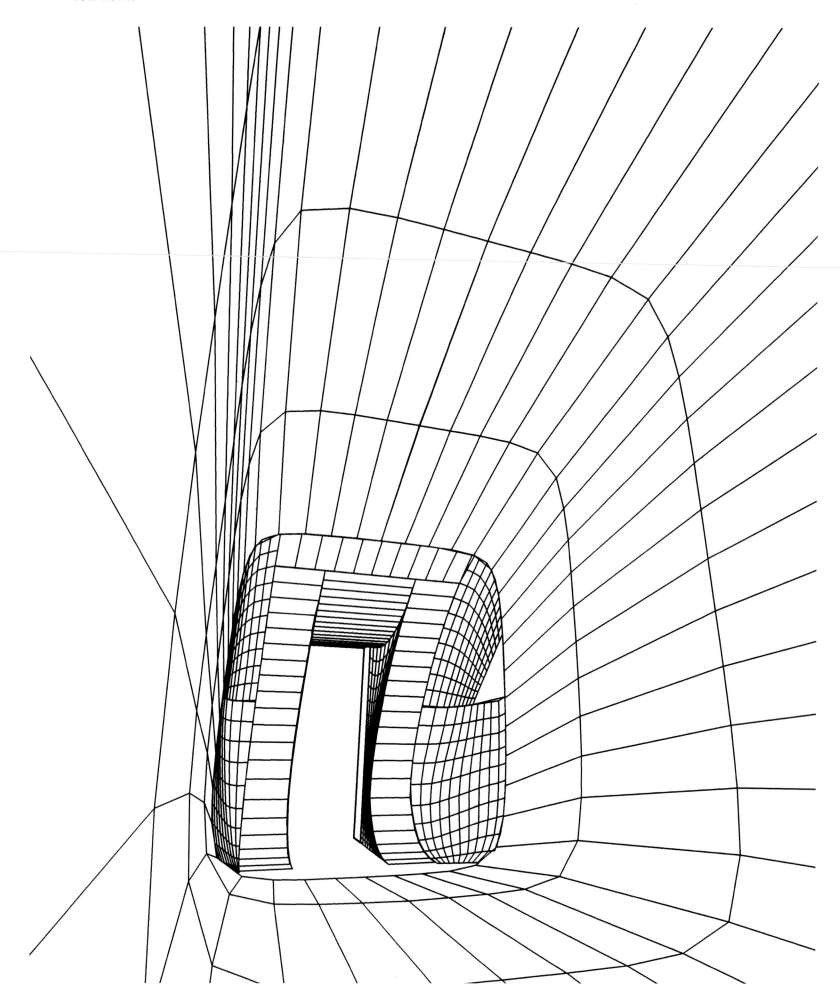

Computer-generated nets showing the development of form and space

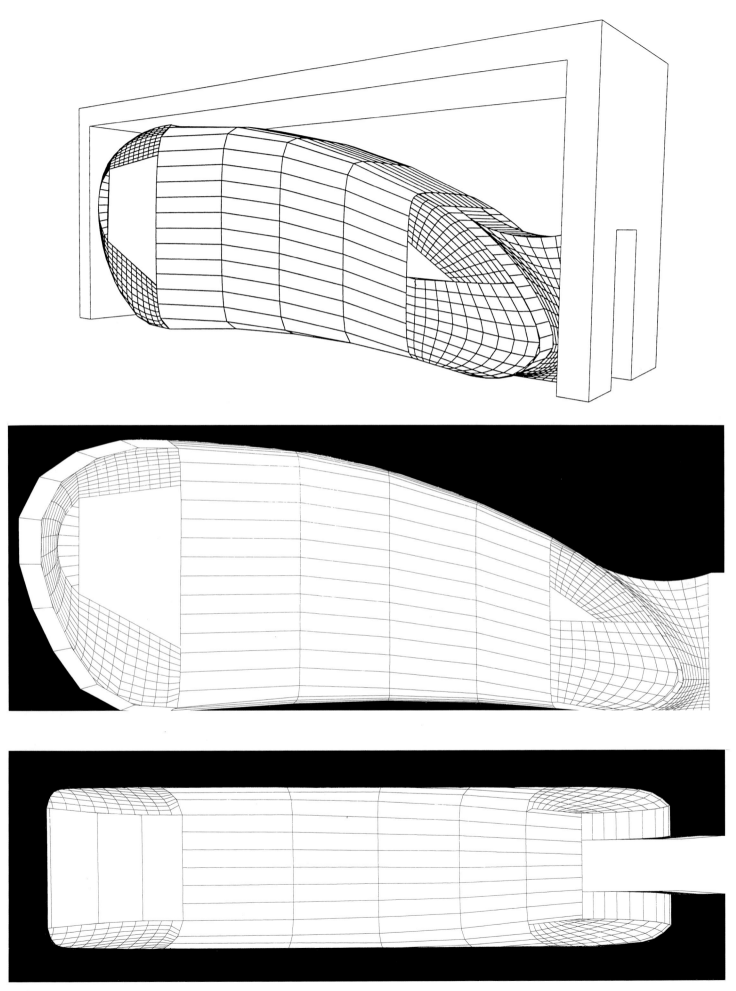

FROM ABOVE: Perspective; section; and plan

Melbourne
Sapore Restaurant
1995

The Sapore Restaurant is a creation within an existing two-storey building overlooking Port Philip Bay in St Kilda. The project addresses the external promenade, and the sweeping boulevard is a key focus in framing the view into and from the restaurant. The facade of the Victorian building was preserved, but the floor-to-ceiling height at ground level was reduced to 2.1 metres. This unusually low ceiling intensifies the experience of entering the double-height dining space, which opens up into a deceptively large volume. This expansive, fluid volume is anchored by an existing beam which forms a bridge connecting the ground- and first-level dining areas. The spatial complexity of the ground floor is generated by an interplay of solid elements, concealed stairs and other utilities that are contained within the wrapped white skin that lines the space. The spare white ceiling opens on to two deep elliptical spaces, which visually link the two floors and provide natural light. The central ground-floor space is grounded by a black concrete bar, which arrests its fluid surrounds. The extra spaces between the utility areas and the existing stairs were filled with a stretched skin. This made the limitations of the existing structure and the new envelope increasingly free from functional determinations. The fluid sculptural result was achieved by playing with the forms on site and developing the geometry in a very immediate and real way.

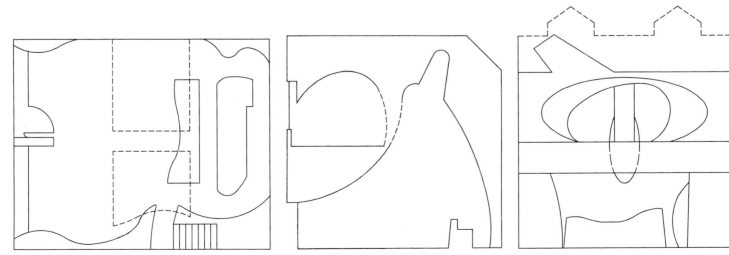

Outline plan and sections

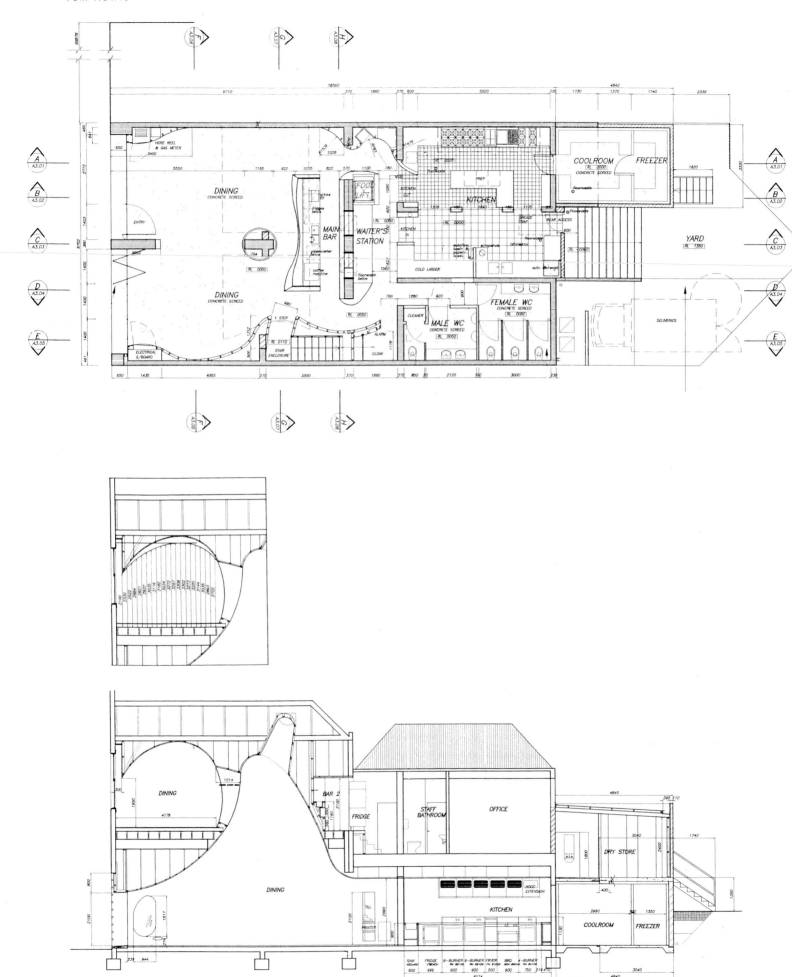

FROM ABOVE: Ground floor plan; detail for ceiling construction; section AA (working drawing)

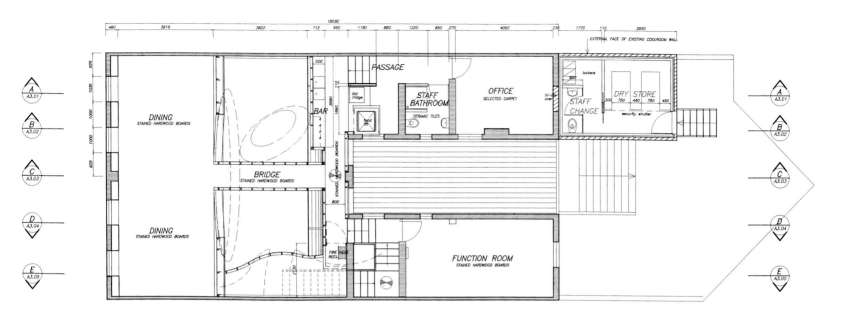

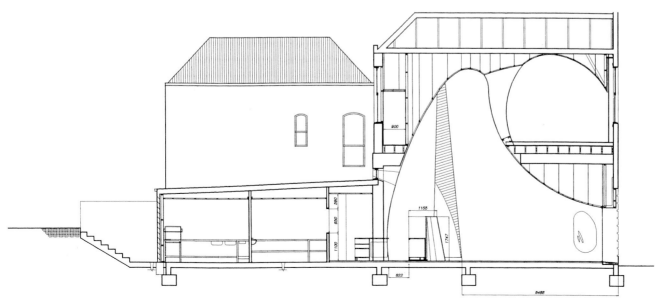

FROM ABOVE: First floor plans; section DD (working drawings)

FROM ABOVE, LEFT TO RIGHT: Ground floor restaurant; view of bridge from below; view to bridge access

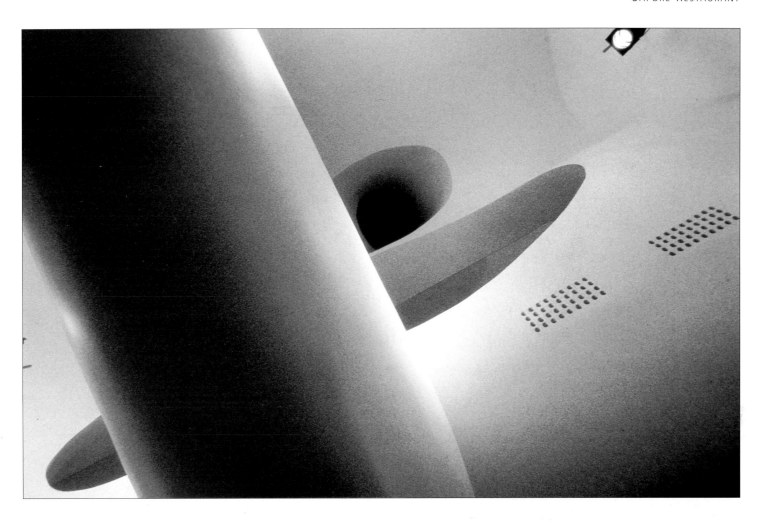

FROM ABOVE: Bridge and skylight detail; entrance view to restaurant

Melbourne
Ryan Studio
1995

Located in Melbourne's city fringe, the Ryan Studio is inserted into an existing factory shell. The client's brief asked for an integrated living/work station, which could function as a living zone within the warehouse. The solution was the insertion of an open pod-like form that accentuates the difference between old and new. The structure squeezes and surrounds itself in the narrow environment – articulating a spatial experience that breaks the bounds of the existing rectilinear pattern. Perceived as a solid, incommensurable form, the pod contains the functional living requirements of the artist, intensifying a total working process. The stairwell substrata contains the kitchen and utility areas, while the level above contains the sleeping zone. The bedroom aperture brings in natural light and extends itself to the outside face of the west facade. It is the only external sign of a new addition to the building. Fluidity of form asserts itself through a plaster surface, the white volume of which extends against the existing red brickwork and concrete floor.

As a juxtaposition, the pod is a contextual response in both material and form. It creates a form as an entity containing, while at the same time addressing, its political stance from within.

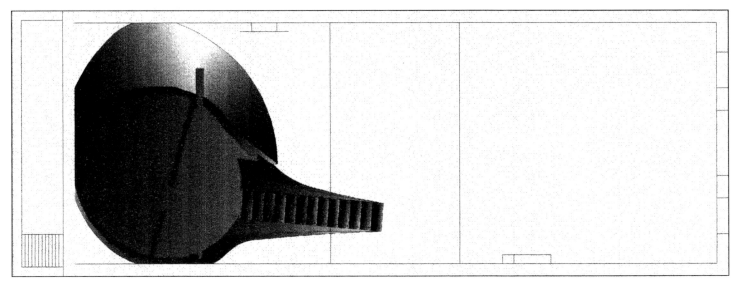

OPPOSITE: Stair to bedroom
ABOVE: Computer-generated image of inserted form

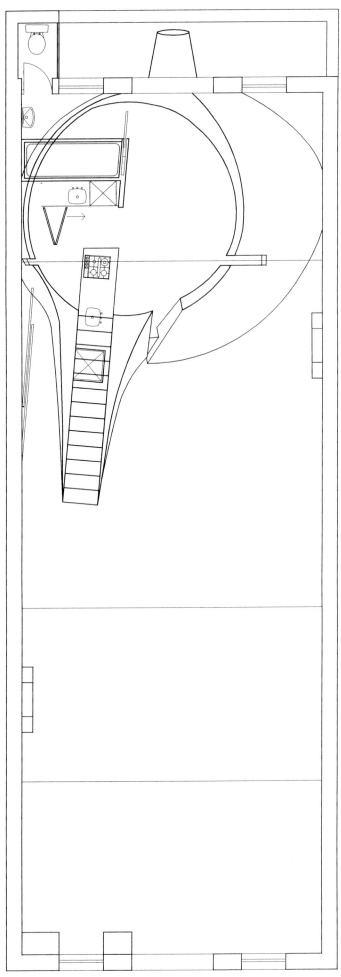

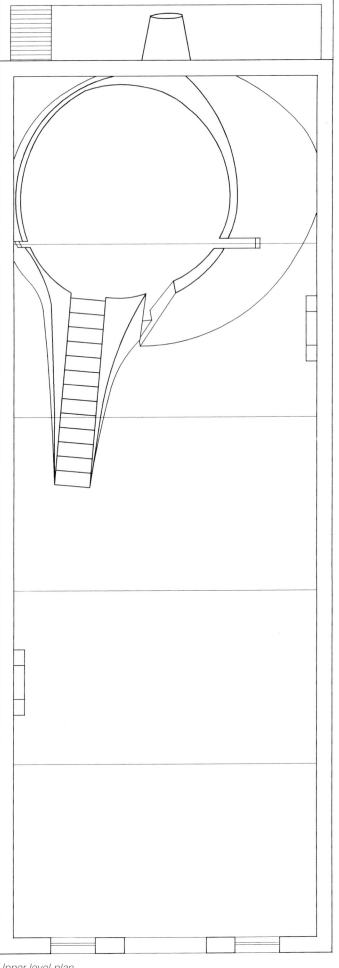

Lower level plan

Upper level plan

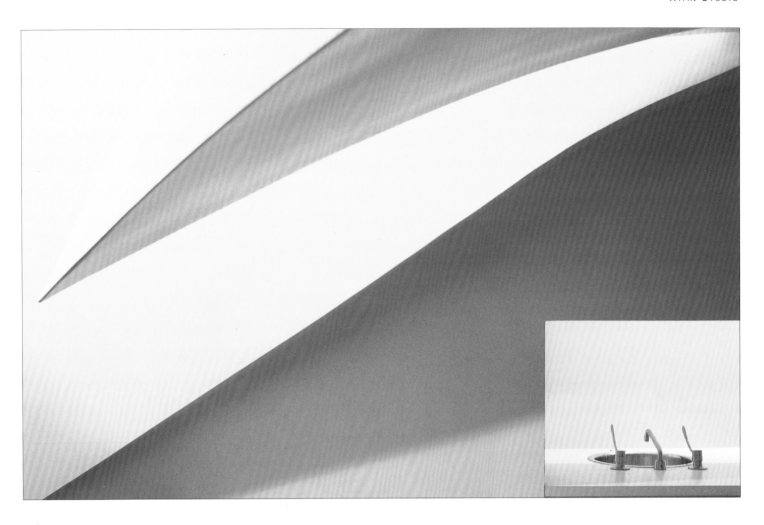

FROM ABOVE: Stair and kitchen detail; view of inserted pod from studio entrance

Melbourne Atlas House 1996

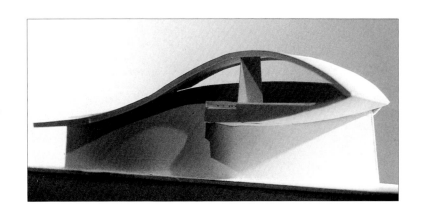

The Atlas House is a 350-square-metre residence built on the edge of public parkland in Hawthorn, a suburb of Melbourne. It has a mixture of semi-public areas for entertaining and private areas for the residents.

The house includes an ancillary zone, which accommodates a doctor's surgery, lap pool and utility areas, within the thickness of the wall facing the parkland that spans the length of the site. The central living space is entered through a narrow passage, which also functions as a dividing zone between the private bedroom wing and the expanse of the entertaining area. The western aspect of the building – which in Australia is traditionally shielded from the harsh sunlight – is the pivotal one. It directs the living aspect into a courtyard

and extends the building line. It also acts as a buffer from the park and freeway beyond. The internal spaces frame the views through narrow vertical openings in the thickness of the walls. They function as formal devices which define the grounded mass as a single object.

It was intended that the house would have a civic reading, an edge, and would define itself against the existing fabric of the suburban blur. Its sweeping form bends the statutory planning codes and addresses the conventional modes of production. The mass of the street frontage is maintained at a minimum height to allow minimum distance from the boundary. Maximum height is achieved in the living zone by canting the walls. This is gradually lowered at the front and rear to meet building codes.

The formal reading of the building was achieved partly through resistance to outmoded planning and building codes and a pragmatic response to the client's requirements. Materials were selected to express the plastic nature of the form. Render surface was used on the outside walls and fibreglass lining was used for the roof. This method produced a denser reading of the house. Traditional details were pared back, and fragmentation of form caused by additional material and texture removed. The relationship between interior and exterior is fused with the use of white plaster in the interior forms. The house is defined by its urban composition, in form, scale and the spatial consideration of the design brief, and the contextual condition of the site.

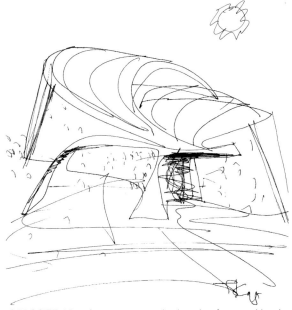

OPPOSITE: View from street; north elevation from parkland
ABOVE: Preliminary sketch

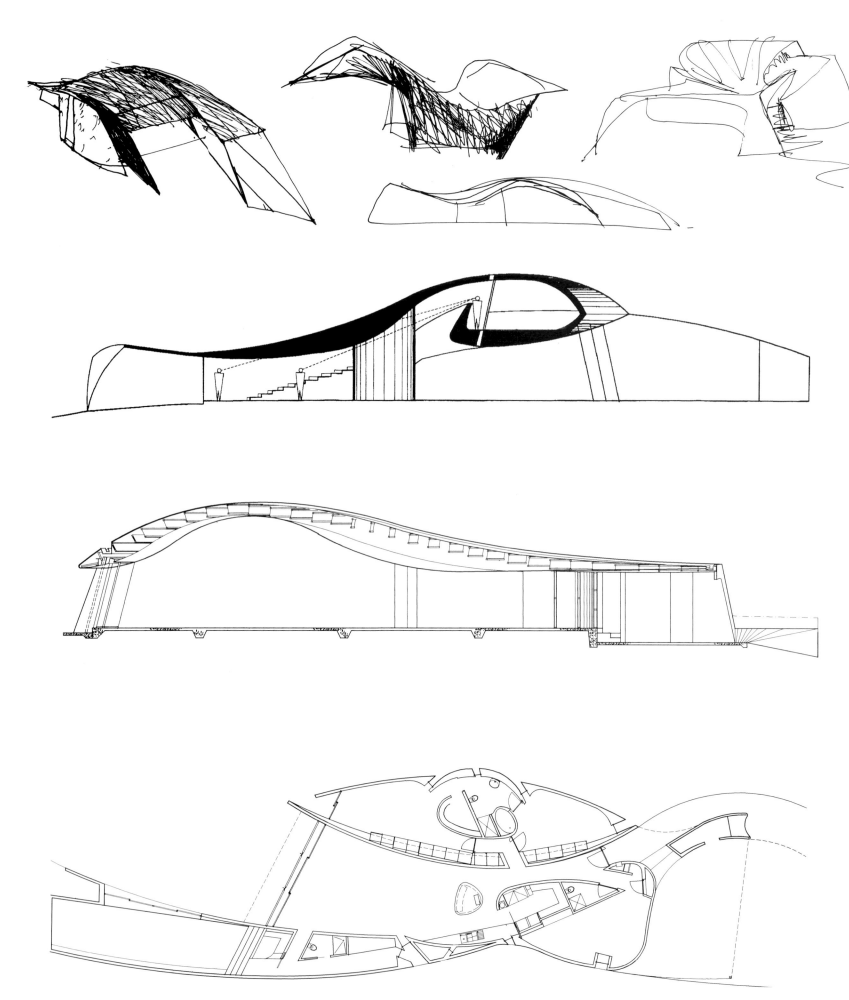

FROM ABOVE: Conceptual sketches; longitudinal section; section through living area and entrance hall; ground level plan

FROM ABOVE: Front entrance; construction detail of living area

Melbourne
Urban Attitude
1996

This retail outlet for domestic wares was developed for a client who wished to go beyond the limits of conventional store design. The new 150-square-metre space was intended to be flexible with a distinct visual and spatial image.

The spatial intervention wraps through the existing interior walls with a single unfolding gesture of service counter and display shelving. Embracing the volume with a strange sense of perspective, the architecture is a commentary on limits, reduction and movement through a carved white space. Conceived on site from an original sketch, importance was placed on the immediacy of the moment, and the feeling created from the space. The plastic form of the interior is organised around a continuous coherent form with curving shelves that act as an ordering device for the evolution of the fluid spatial injection. The use of plaster was dictated by the brief and budget. The spatial coherence arises out of the need to emphasise the scale of the space as a vessel for the merchandise on display. Shoppers move through the store in a rotational movement imposed by the plan, a device which allows architecture to be experienced through a tactile and visual relationship with the space.

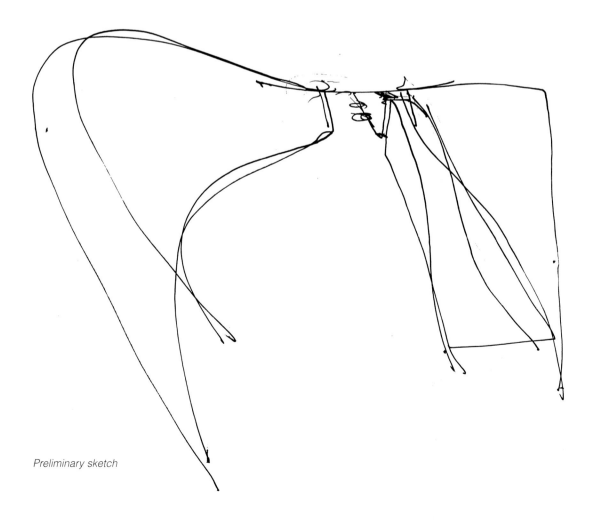

Preliminary sketch

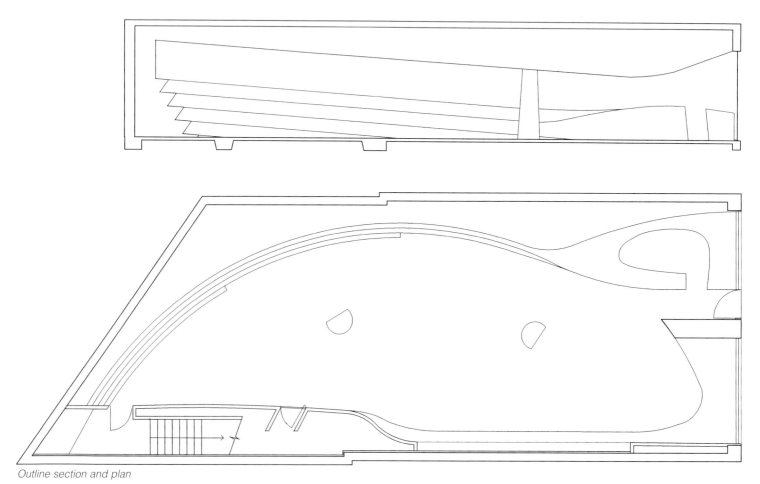

Outline section and plan

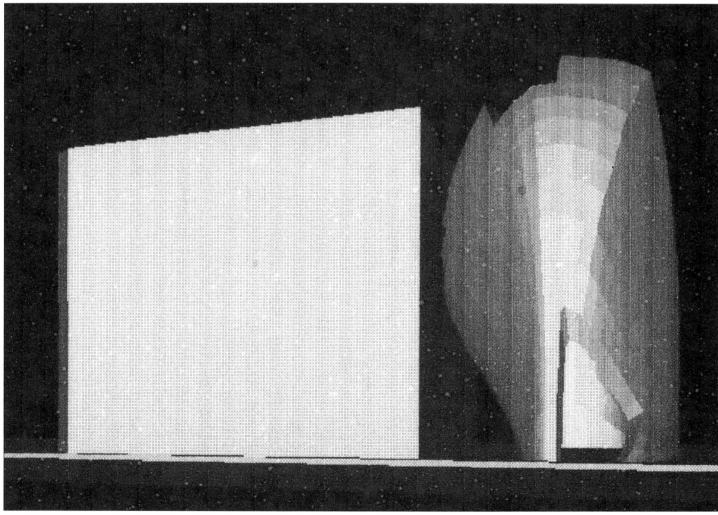

Melbourne
Barkly Apartments
1996

The Barkly Apartments project is for a commercial/residential infill building in the seaside area of St Kilda, Melbourne. Wedged in a narrow site, it provides car access and parking facilities at ground level. The ground template is distorted and expands vertically to accommodate the apartment envelope above. Experienced as a changing and growing form, the building is compressed at ground level but rises and expands into a large mass.

At ground level the entrance leads to a long staircase. Natural light filters into this narrow rise which opens to the apartments on all four levels through glass panels, allowing light to penetrate the depth of the passage and stairwell. Apartments extend longitudinally across the site focusing the living areas towards the main street, with filtered light entering from concealed overhead openings, emphasising a dialectic between the hidden and the revealed.

The generating principle of the building attempts to subvert the orthogonal nature of the site and extend its limits into a maximum volume to capitalise on the available land area and natural light. Space is manipulated in the depth of the building to accommodate the functional requirements, while avoiding fragmenting the form of the whole. Emphasis is placed on expressing the solid physical quality of the object and articulating the building as a volume which brings the collective spaces to their simplest formal expression. The strict budget required a membrane finish which would enable an economic construction and allow the building volume to be read as a clear and defined solid object.

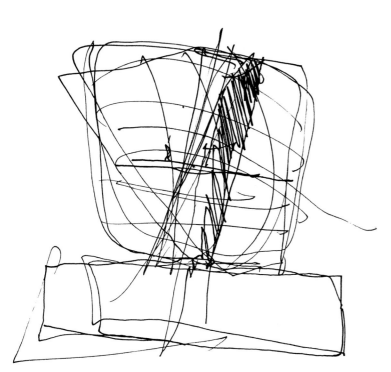

OPPOSITE: Aerial view; front elevation – computer-generated studies of form
ABOVE: Preliminary study

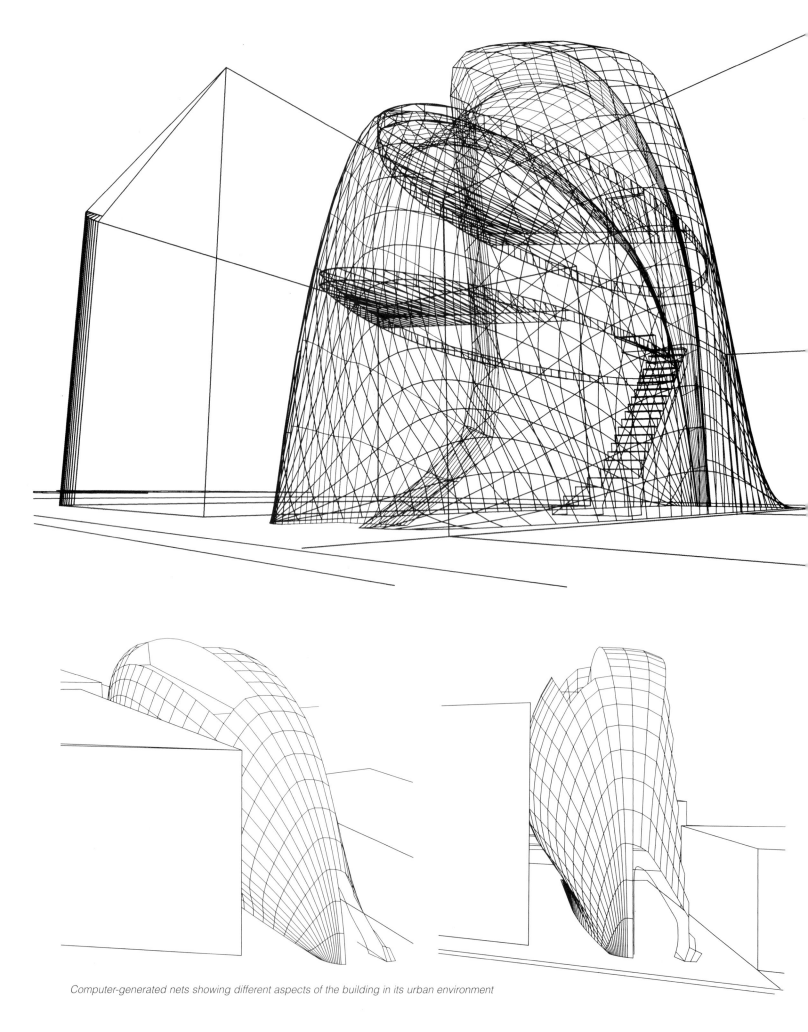

Computer-generated nets showing different aspects of the building in its urban environment

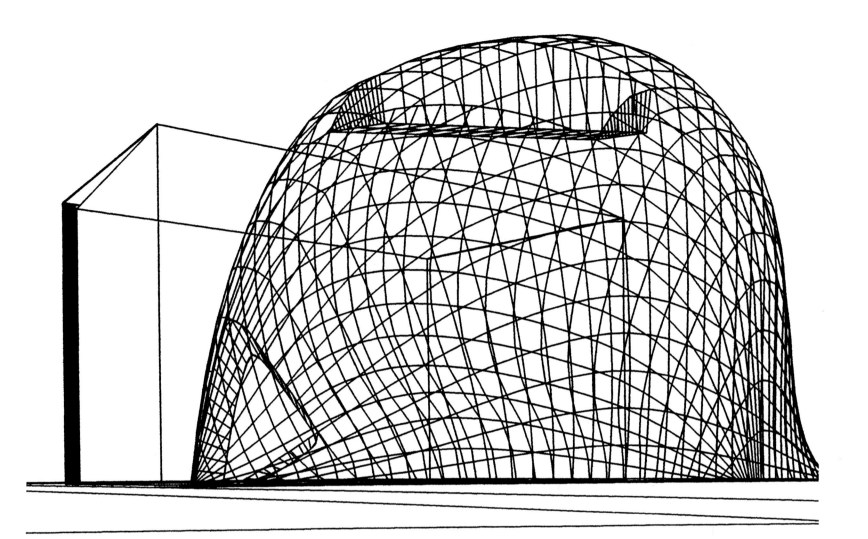

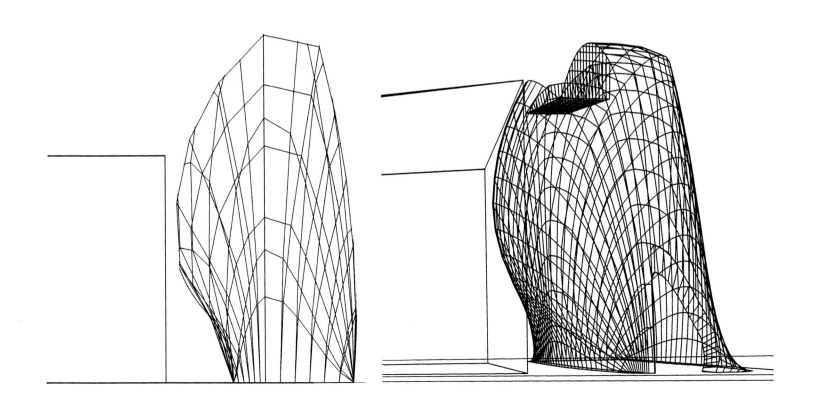

Computer-generated net of building in context

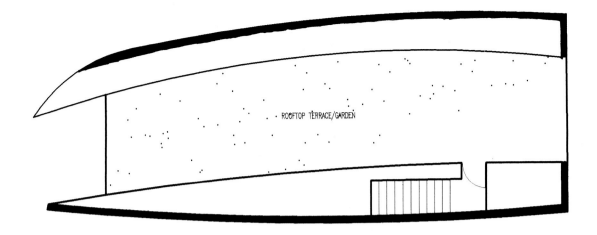

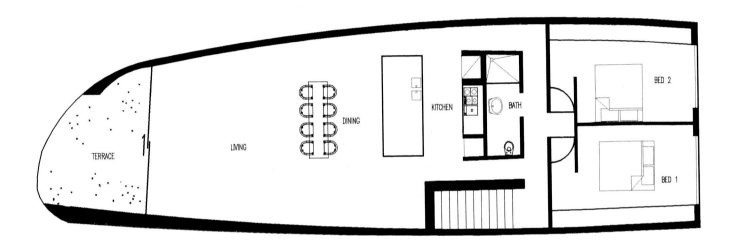

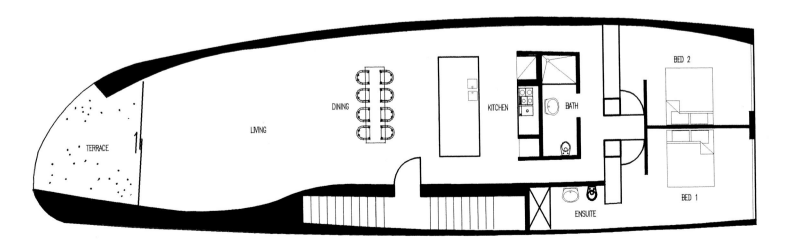

FROM ABOVE: Roof plan; second floor plan; first floor plan

Melbourne
Pless House
1996

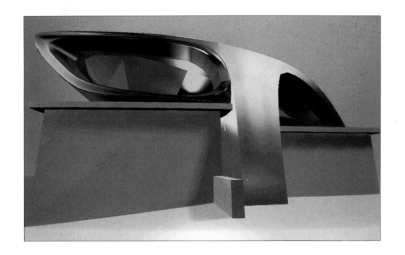

Occupying a corner site in the tree-lined suburb of Toorak, Melbourne, this project is for a new roof-top residence above a modernist house built in the sixties. Construction is about to begin at the time of writing, and is due to be completed in 1998.

The client wanted a building with a distinct visual identity which also optimised land use and potential views of the city. Conceived as an independent form, though adjoining the existing house, it provided an opportunity to extend conventional design vocabulary. The new building is made up of three elements which are clustered around a central vertical distribution core, off which the bedrooms and living area are composed into a single mass. The exterior is surfaced in treated zinc panels to produce an extremely sculptural form. Internal spaces become extruded externally and are an extension of the conceptual intent.

The house set out to bend the planning codes and overcome the many objections from the neighbours. Building setbacks and height restrictions were accepted as part of the creative process and partly determined the final object, establishing a response and a scale that was appropriate to the urban context.

The main facade, which overlooks the street, responds to the scale and height of existing houses, while avoiding the fragmentation and staggering of its neighbours. The windows and continuity in the horizontal pattern are a response to the building below, which is used as a pattern for offsetting the walls. Such bending of codes and conventions is a means of expanding the design process.

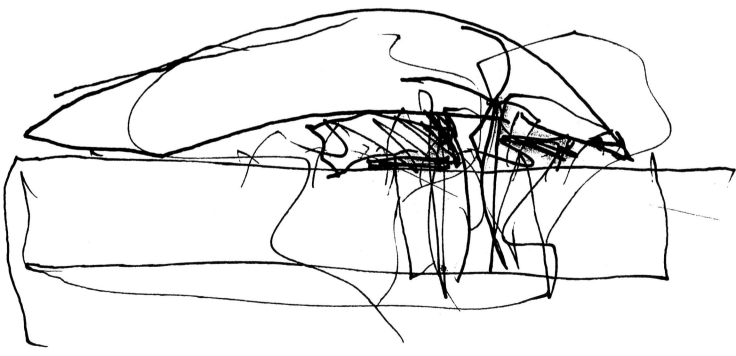

Conceptual sketch

Tom Kovac

Detail of a sheet of
conceptual sketches

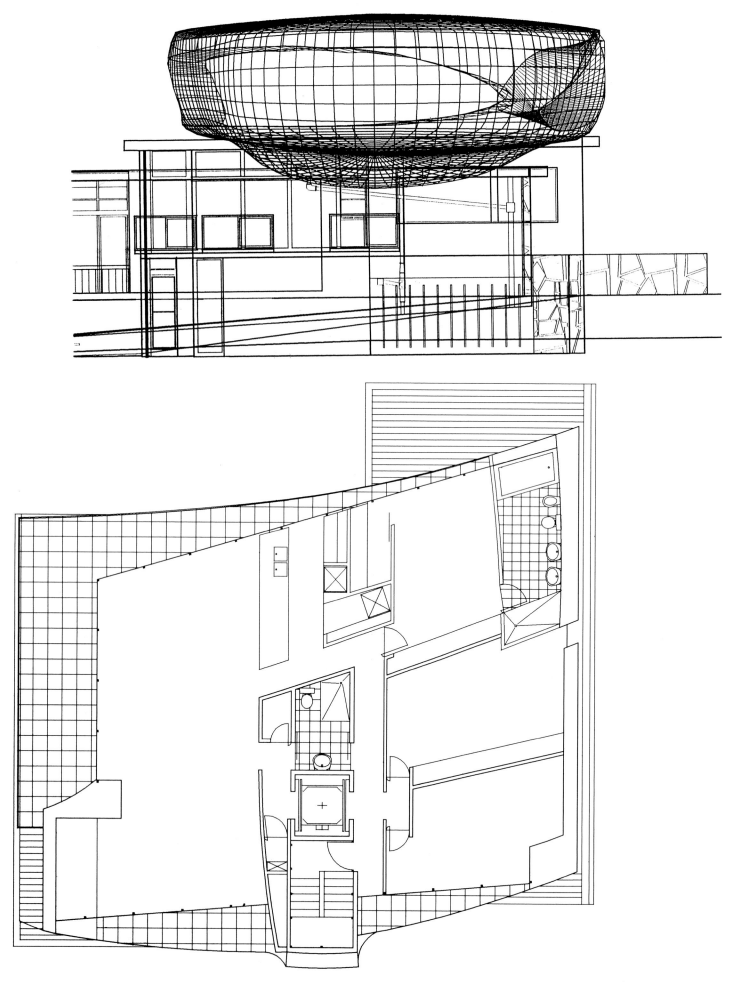

FROM ABOVE: computer-generated net showing modelling of addition on existing house; plan

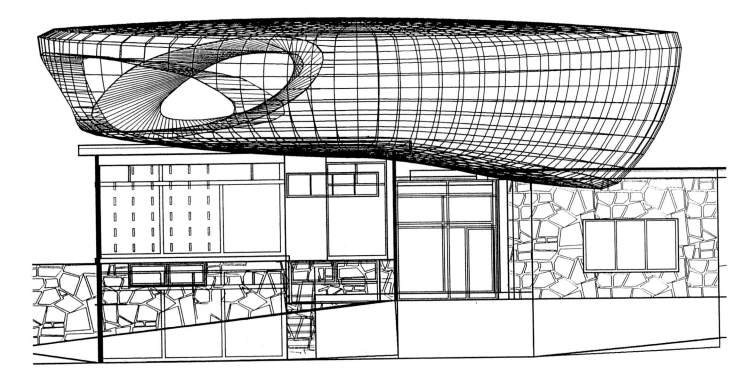

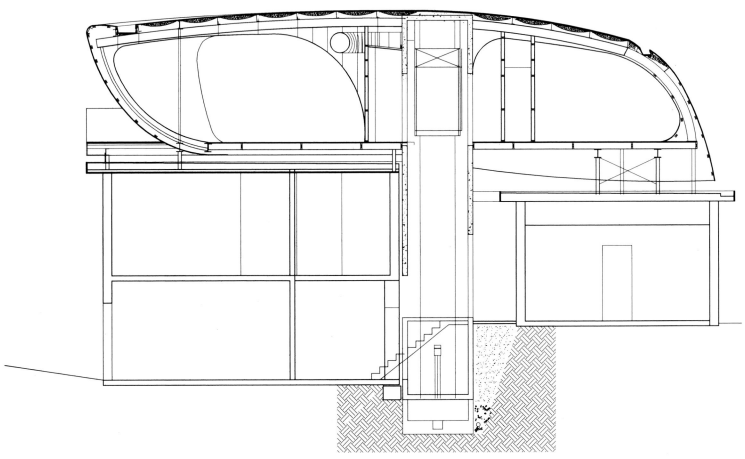

FROM ABOVE: Computer generated net showing modelling of addition on existing house; section

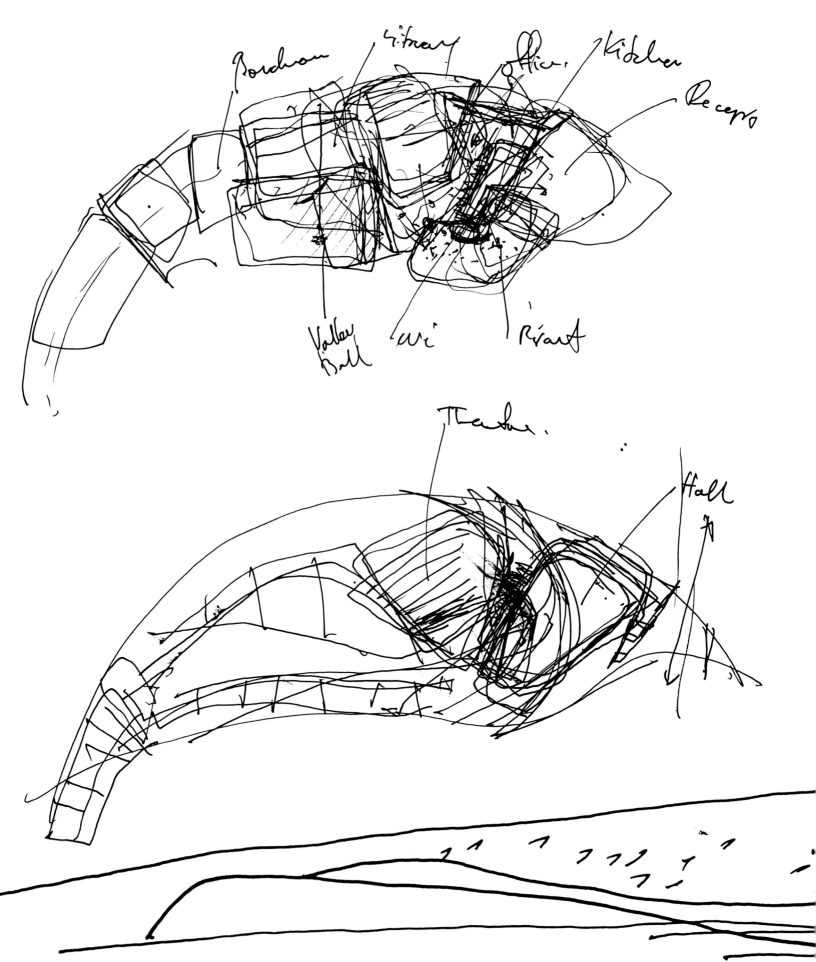

Preliminary sketches of plan forms and elevation

Melbourne
Pontian Centre
1996

This project was produced for an invited competition that sought to establish a cultural centre for Melbourne. The brief called for the retention of an existing football field, and the creation of an auditorium for lectures and theatre productions, a restaurant, a student sports centre, community rooms, a library and a children's centre. The site is unusual for such a facility in that it is located amongst industrial warehouses and factories overlooking a railway line.

The isolation of the building became the stimulus for the design solution and Kovac's approach to the urban setting. Parking facilities are located directly off the main road, and the building is conceived as a single form dividing the rear outdoor sports area from the front. The main entrance to the building is addressed as the focal point for the gathering and distribution of visitors. Rather than fragmenting, it made sense to gather the centre in a single form containing the different functions.

This creates a clear presence and scale for the cultural centre within the industrial zone. It has a two-level form, which divides the project into two zones. The ground level contains the facilities which require public access, and the first level consists of an auditorium and bar. As a vertical central space the interior grounds the mass and unifies the site. The exterior reads as a large curving object which extends over the site and creates a protective boundary.

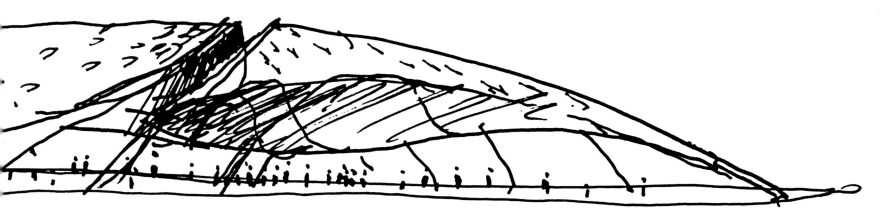

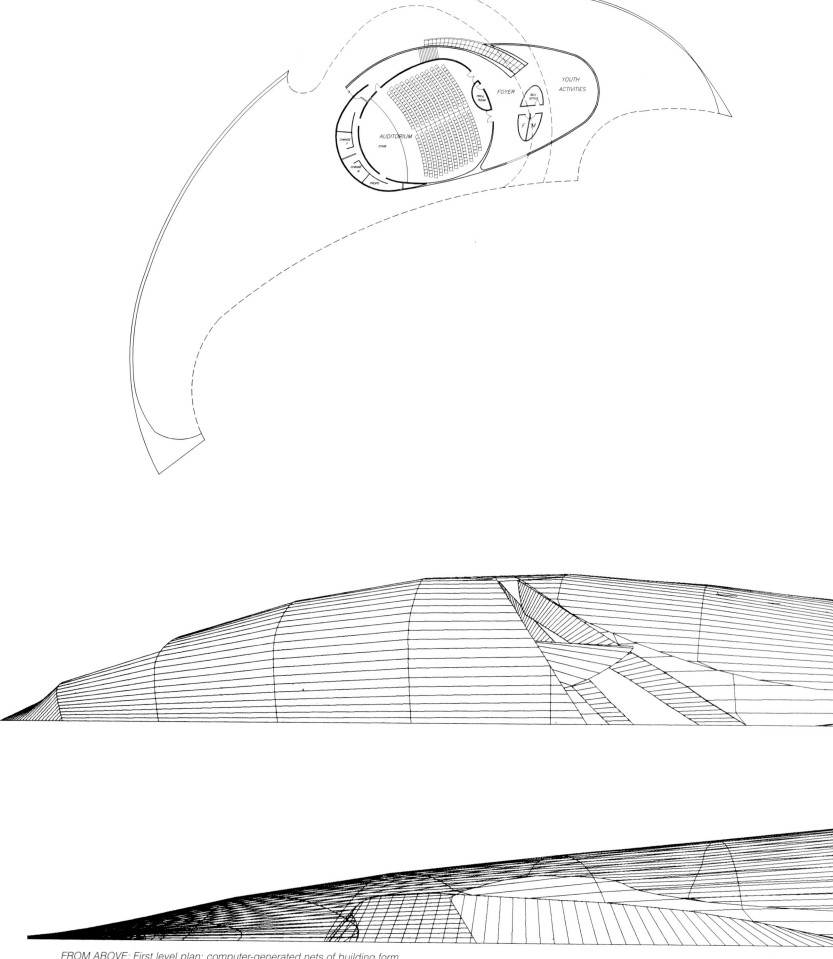

FROM ABOVE: First level plan; computer-generated nets of building form

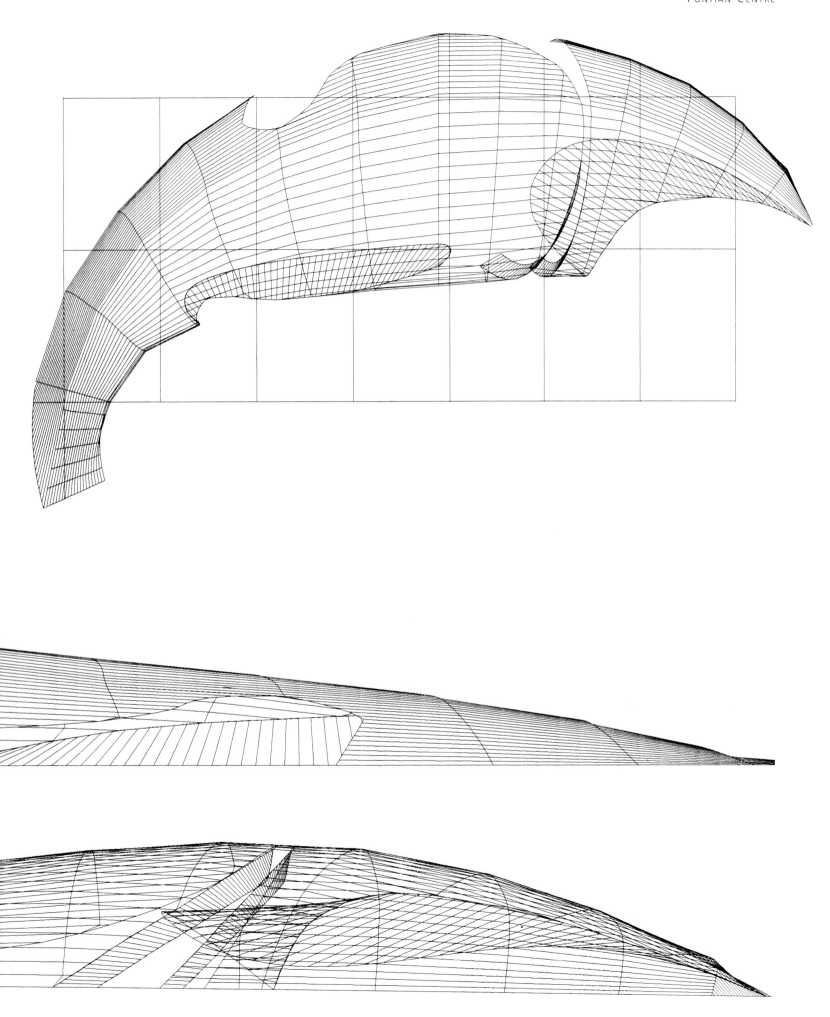

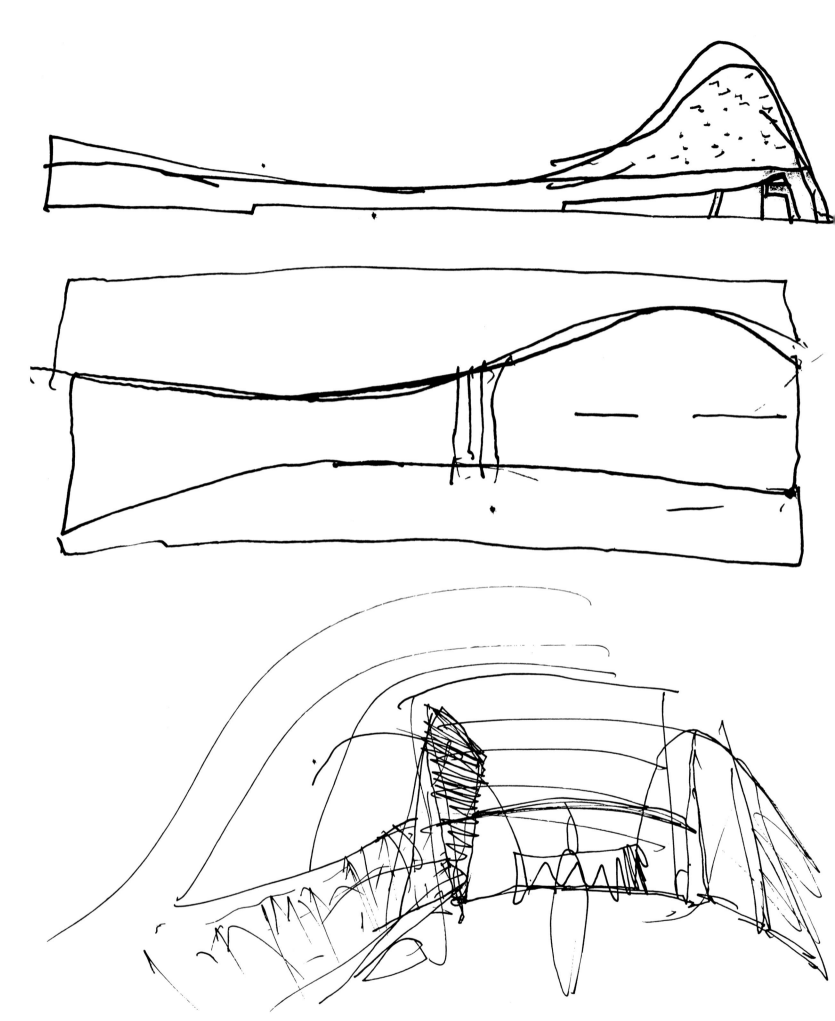

Preliminary sketches

Sydney
Tonic
1997

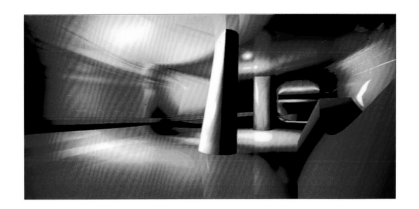

This project is located in a strategic site on the main strip of Oxford Street, Sydney, within the ground floor of the Holiday Inn Hotel. The space extends from the main frontage through to the rear courtyard, which has amazing views across the city. Due for completion in 1997, it is centred around a programme to establish a restaurant/bar and kitchen area within the existing restaurant space.

The site is long and narrow, and is restricted by ceiling heights and existing services. Kovac's scheme is dominated by a complex and continuous internal skin that extends from the front facade through to the rear, gathering the walls and ceiling in an undulating gesture to reshape the interior into a new formal insertion.

The space reads like a dynamic spatial extrusion, grounded by two bars and an extension that projects into the rear courtyard of the twenty-five storey hotel. Ceilings rise from 2.4 metres to a maximum height of 5 metres at the rear. The front area functions as a bar, with the restaurant extending from the narrow central corridor into the rear. With its sculpted white mass and composition of arcs and folds, the project fuses the two separate areas into a single, clear and defined volume.

Produced in association with Dale Jones-Evans Pty Ltd

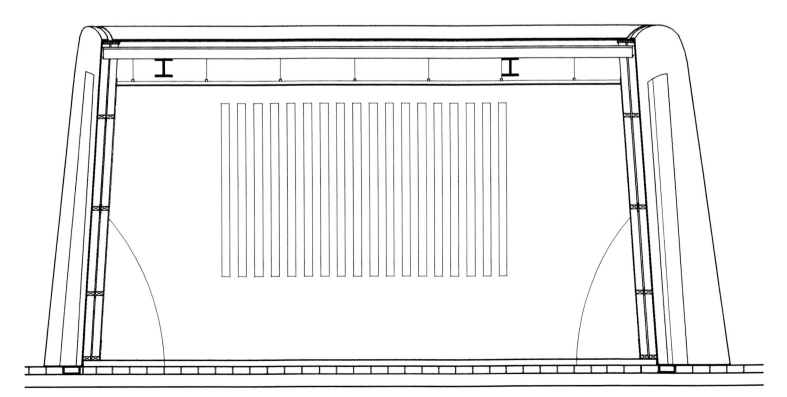

Part section

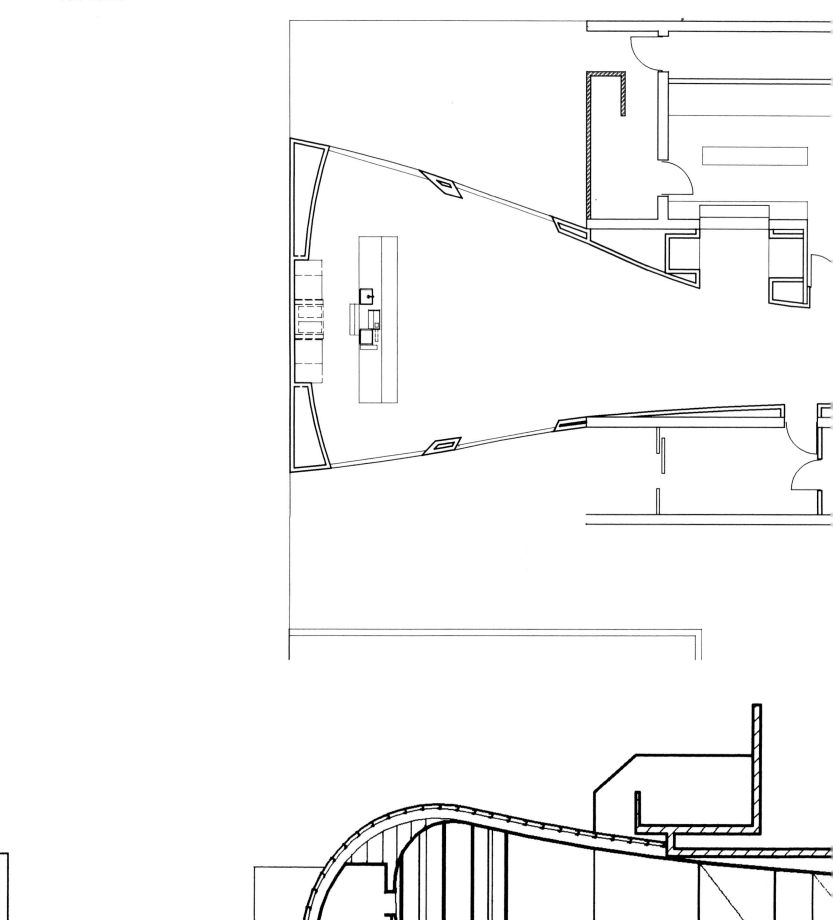

FROM ABOVE: Floor plan; longitudinal section

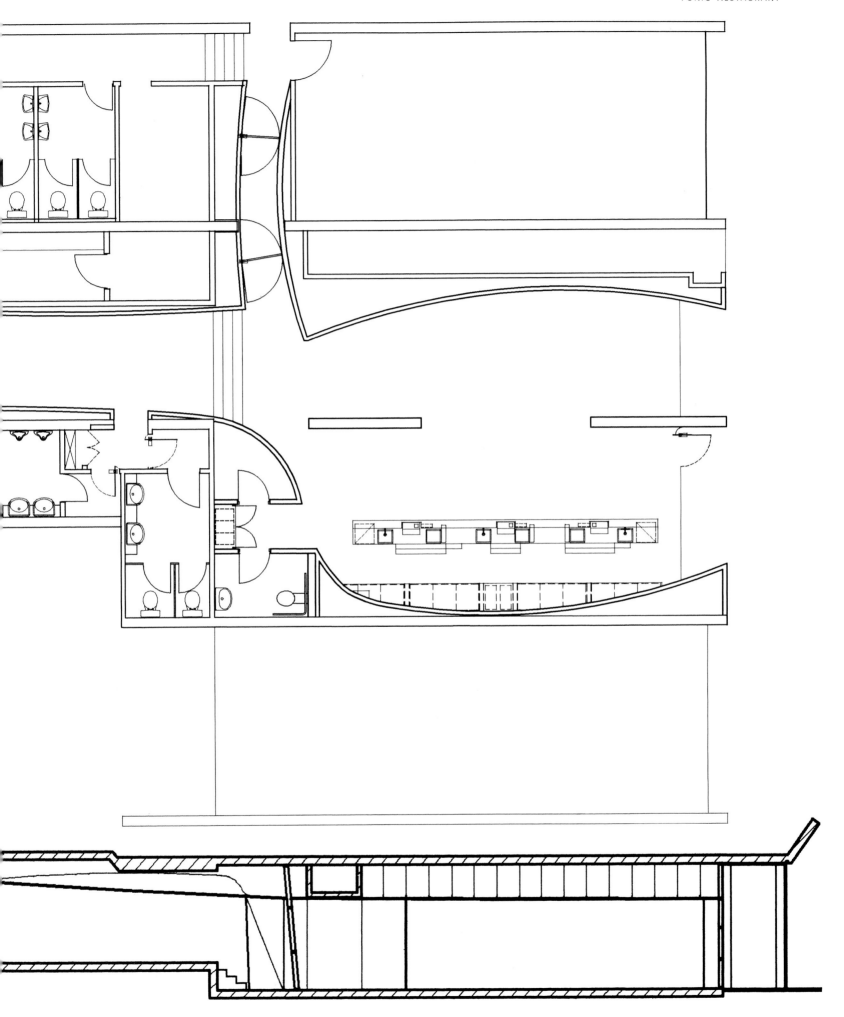

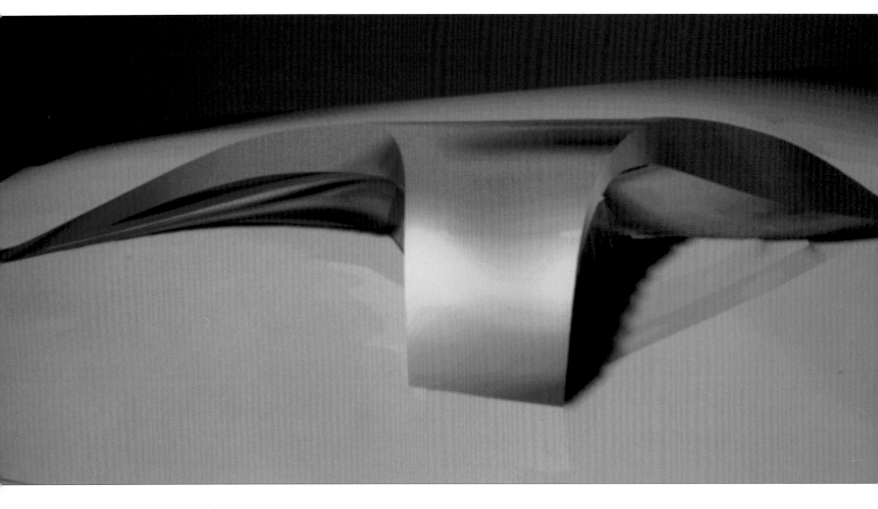

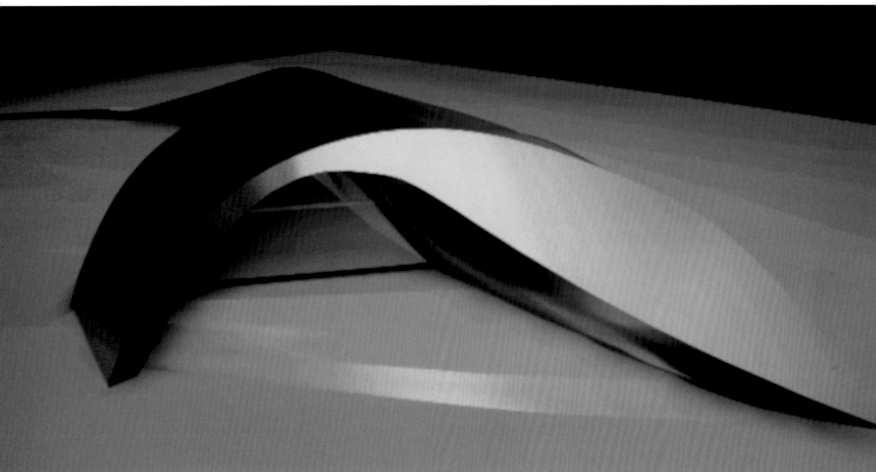

Victoria Island House 1997

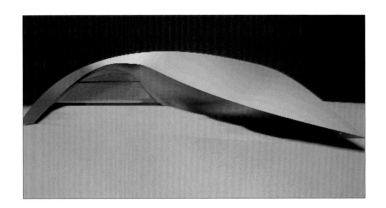

The site for this new house is on French Island, Westerport Bay, Victoria. Situated upon a rising, the clearing has protection from prevailing winds and spectacular views across the ocean. The building includes a main private wing for sleeping and work, and a living zone which is contained within an extended space outside the main form. The sweeping sculptural gesture of the house is conceived as an intervention and composition of complex curved elements which have a plastic formalism re-integrating the land with the house. The special aspect of the site is the vast open spine of the hill and it is this powerful topography which drives the composition. In a sense it is not architecture but nature that makes the essential contribution and defines the plan. The form that emerges is an artificial one, and is dominated by a central body which has a continuous curved mass. Its main entrance is recessed, cut into the hilltop that descends into a passage distributing the private and public circulation of the house. Bedrooms receive natural daylight and ventilation through deep narrow openings in the roof extending into the landscape. The house opens into a covered void with large openable glass partitions, which give the living area dramatic views across Port Philip Bay. This interface between volume, surface and space disintegrates a conventional reading of the house, assuming an anonymity that may potentially become a model that 'un-dominates' the land surface.

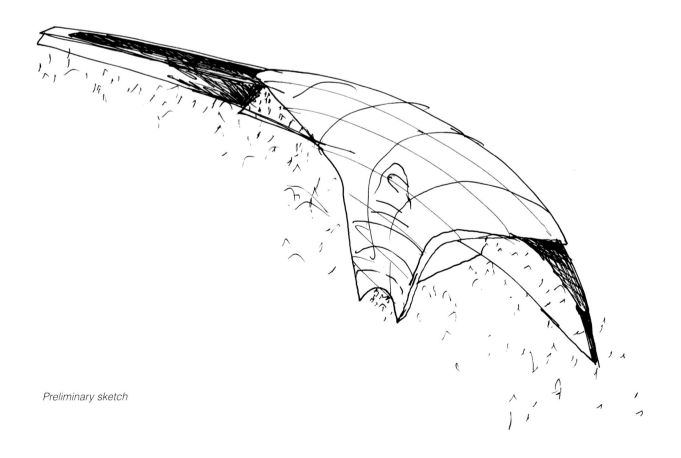

Preliminary sketch

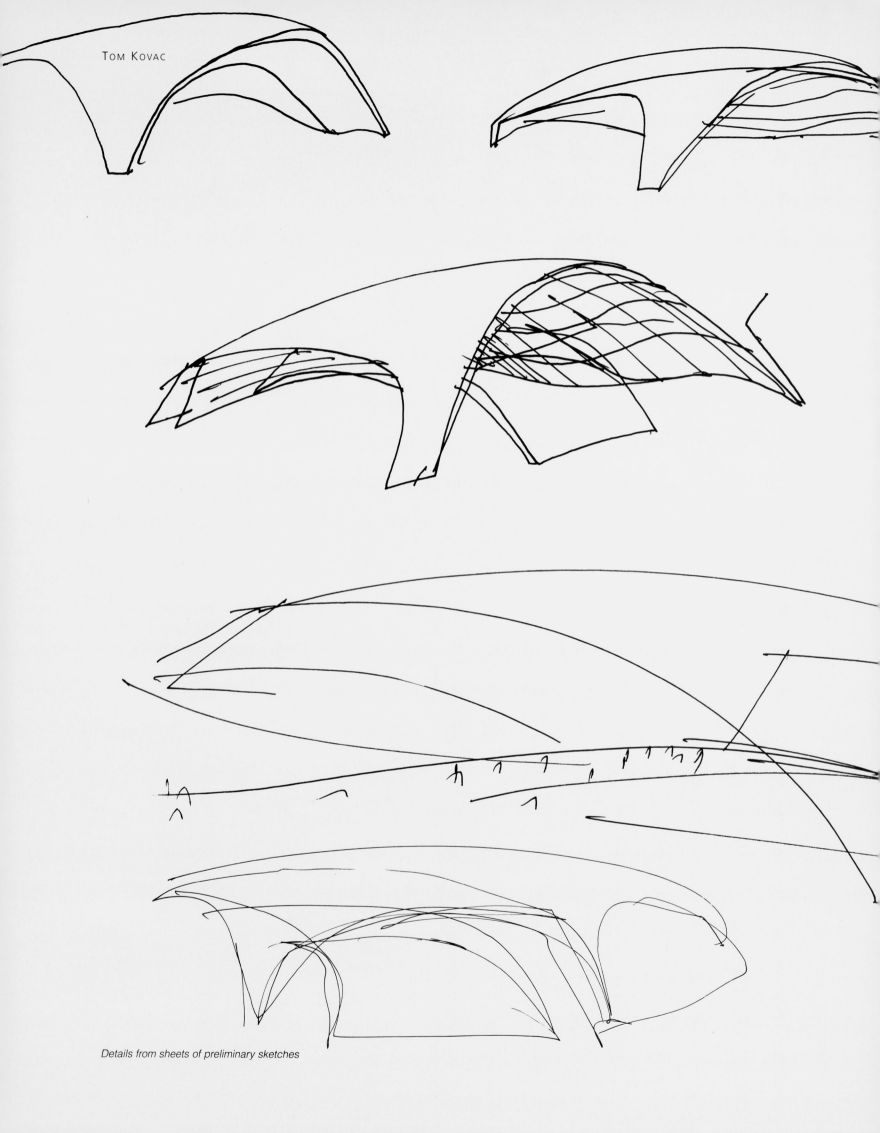

TOM KOVAC

Details from sheets of preliminary sketches

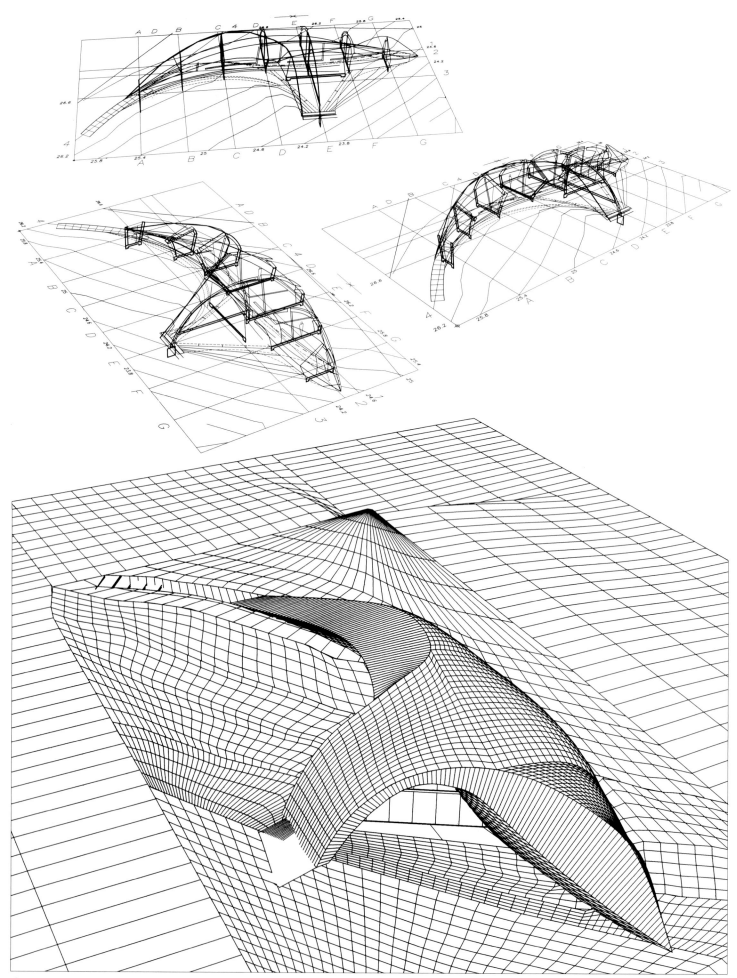

Computer-generated drawings and net showing basic structure and forms

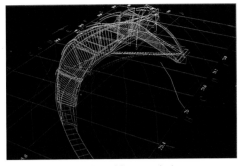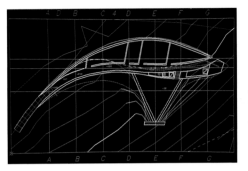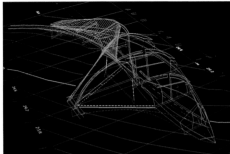

Computer modelling of form and plan

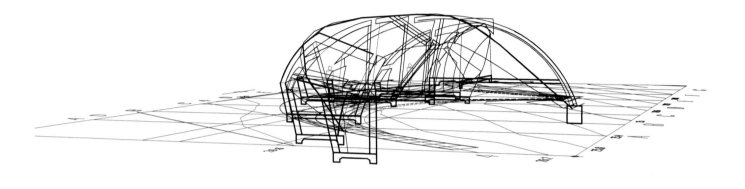

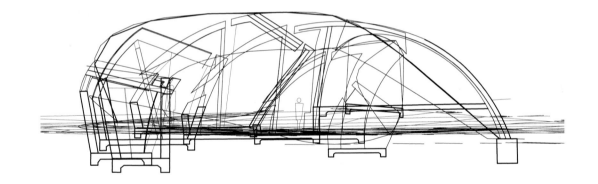

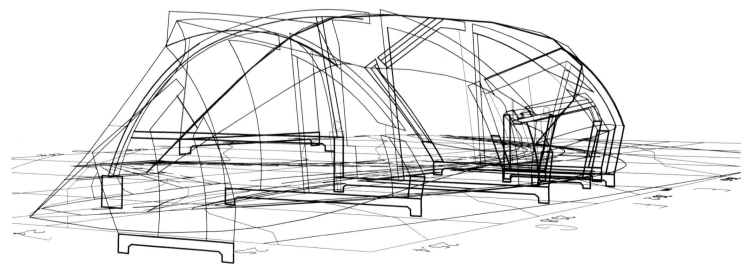

Computer-generated drawings showing basic structure

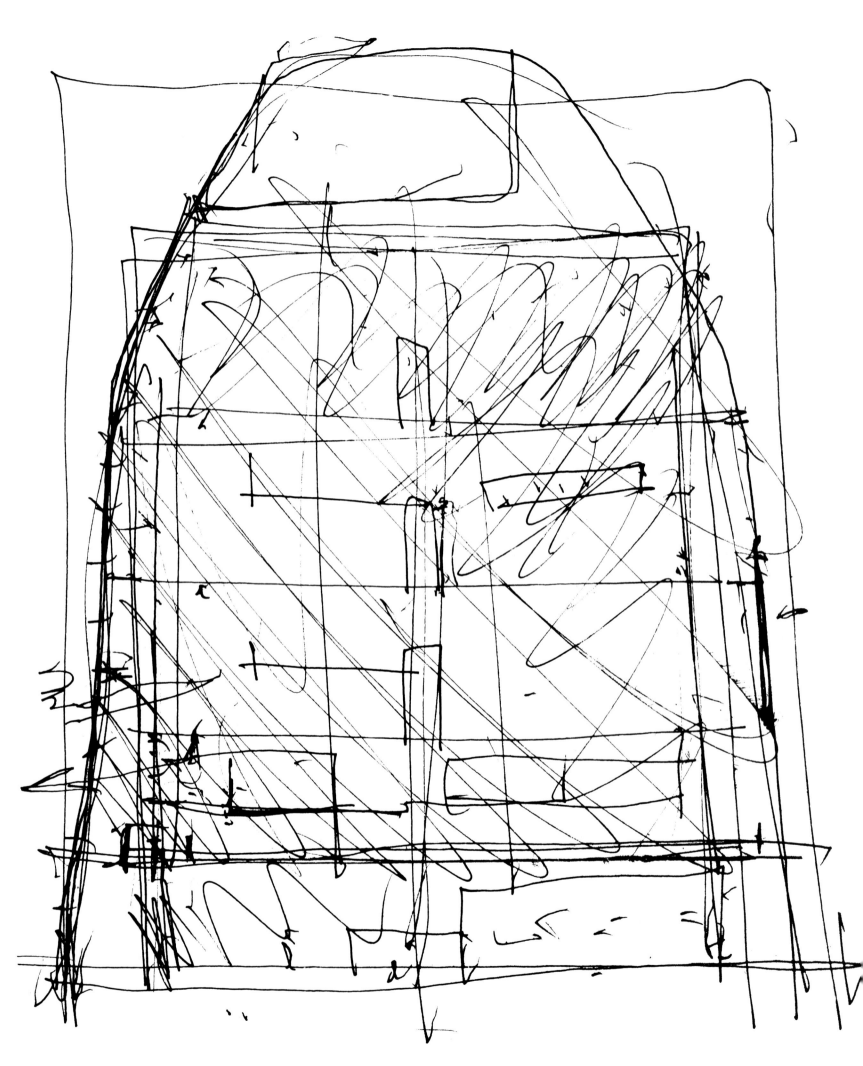

Melbourne
A'Beckett Student Housing
1997

This proposal for student housing is the first comprehensive new redevelopment plan for the area close to the Royal Melbourne Institute of Technology. The street is characterised by continuous planar facades and its distinguishing feature, Edmond and Corrigan's RMIT Building 8, which dominates the skyline to the east of the site.

The scheme is based on clear principles: on reducing the building to its simplest expression and providing accommodation that optimises the space available. The programme requires apartments, a restaurant, an amenities store, a management area, and two basements for car parking. The site density is maximised to accommodate the seven levels necessary to house all the apartments required. A repetitive vertical system is absorbed from the form of the site and this addresses the programme, offering the flexibility to extrude the apartments horizontally and vertically as a uniform system. A central spine is employed to gather the occupants to the centre of the site and distribute vertically. The composition and the repetition of the elevations can be read as a coherent form with the terrace fragments read against a neutral background. The complex has clearly defined edges and avoids the obviousness of reading front, rear and side. Clarity of scale and form defines the building as a separate, abstract entity, separating it from the monotony and fragmentation that otherwise characterises the area.

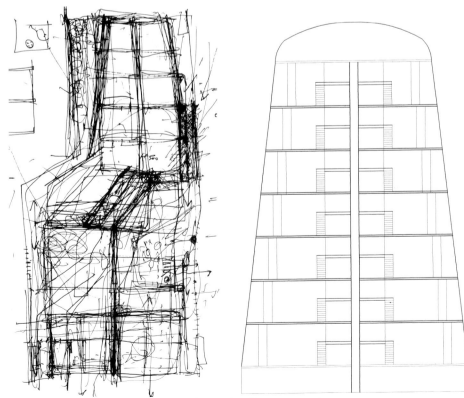

OPPOSITE AND ABOVE: Preliminary sketches and outline cross section

ABOVE LEFT: Computer-generated sections; ABOVE RIGHT: Computer-generated elevations; BELOW: Perspective view

Melbourne Federation Square 1997

This scheme was produced as an entry to the City of Melbourne's international competition for the creation of a major cultural facility on a site previously dominated by two towers. These towers had prevented the area from having a visual connection with the cityscape beyond. The site is bounded by the Flinders Street Railway Station, St Paul's Cathedral and the Yarra River, which defines the city grid. The programme deals with the extension of the site across the existing railway tracks to the river, and a complex accommodating a wintergarden, cinemas, a gallery, commercial facilities and an open public space.

Kovac sought to treat the project as an urban proposition and the architecture as a formal gesture. The lack of coherence in this fragmented area of the city is overcome by using the land formation and existing contours of the site as the anchor for the scheme. The intention was to blur the hard edges between parkland and city, redefining the site's civic focus through contours that are raised as emerging platforms to accommodate activities on three separate levels.

The generating form and its content respond to the scale imposed by the brief, and to the boundaries defining the site. The building is conceived as a series of flexible horizontal land forms growing from the base of the site which evolve into an immaterial vertical gesture. The architecture is experienced through movement and develops as a visual and tactile experience. Composed as a coherent form, the building is perceived as a surface, which has a depth filled by fragmented parts that make up the whole. The continuous ascending platforms also influence the ordering alignments of the new form.

The volumes of the building establish a parallel fenestration along Flinders Street, which is dispersed and lowered towards the river frontage, defining an inner atrium winter garden area. Passage through this landscaped circulation zone extends through the platforms to culminate in a suspended vertical tower overlooking the railway station and the cathedral. This forms a visual connection with Federation Square which articulates the new gateway to the city. In contrast to the buildings surrounding the site, the proposed structure is a light and luminous form. The curvacious platforms are constructed of concrete plates, which are interlaced with ramping systems connecting the levels; the whole is enclosed by a draping glass skin that liberates the space and distinguishes the building from its surroundings. The form dematerialises as it rises and enters a dialogue with the mass of the peripheral edge, redefining the composition of the urban setting.

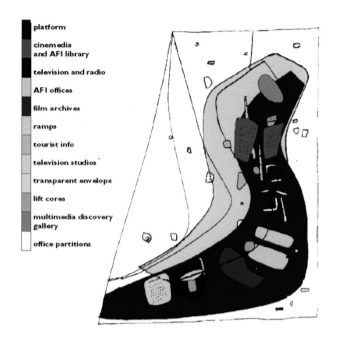

platform

cinemedia
and AFI library

television and radio

AFI offices

film archives

ramps

tourist info

television studios

transparent envelope

lift cores

multimedia discovery
gallery

office partitions

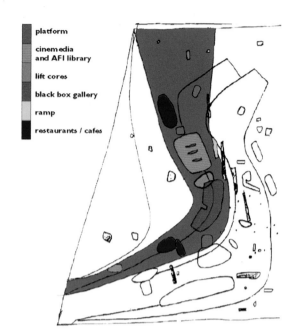

platform

cinemedia
and AFI library

lift cores

black box gallery

ramp

restaurants / cafes

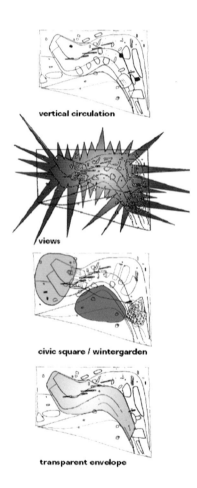

vertical circulation

views

civic square / wintergarden

transparent envelope

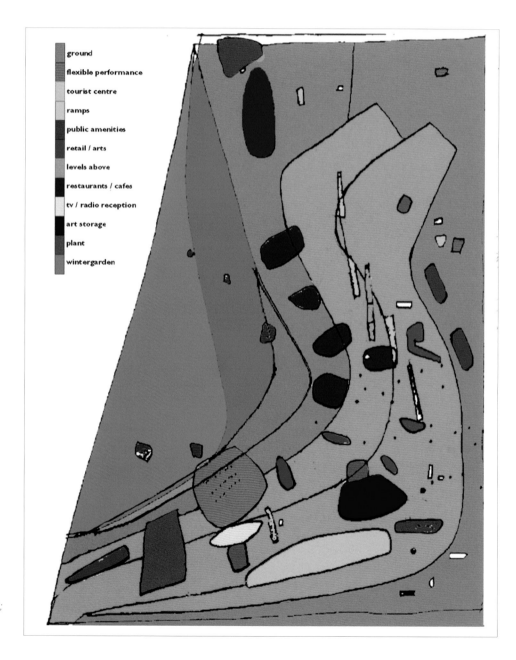

ground

flexible performance

tourist centre

ramps

public amenities

retail / arts

levels above

restaurants / cafes

tv / radio reception

art storage

plant

wintergarden

*ABOVE, LEFT TO RIGHT: Platform 2; platform 1;
BELOW, LEFT TO RIGHT: Concept diagrams;
ground platform*

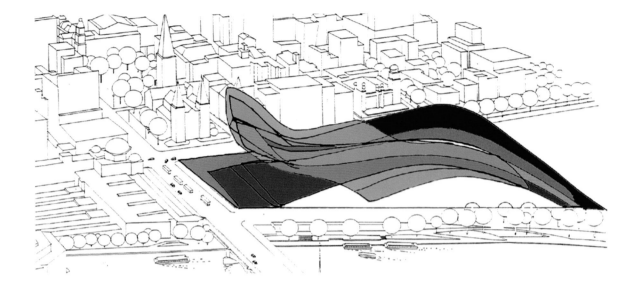

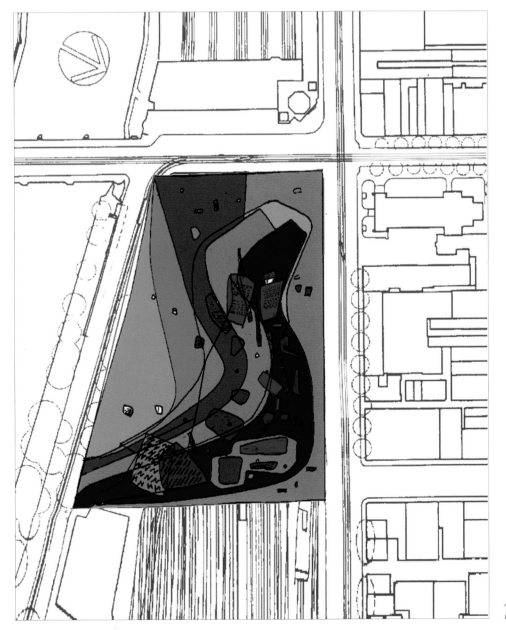

ground
landscape
platform one
platform two
roof platform
transparent envelope
platform two facilities

access

underground access

ABOVE: Isometric view; BELOW, LEFT TO RIGHT: Masterplan, concept diagrams

Biographical Information

1958   Born in Celje, Slovenia
1970   Arrives in Australia (currently resides in Melbourne)

Academic qualifications
1986   Bachelor of Architecture, RMIT
1997   Master of Architecture, RMIT

Professional experience
1987   Editor, *Interior Architecture*
1990   Founds Kovac Architecture
1991   Member Royal Australian Institute of Architects
1994   Founds Curve Architecture Gallery, Melbourne

Academic positions
1992   Lecturer in Design, Faculty of Environmental
          Design and Construction, RMIT
1993   Guest Critic in Design, RMIT
1996   Tutor in Design, RMIT
1997   Tutor in Design, RMIT

Awards
1990   RAIA Winner, Interior Architecture Award
          RAIA Finalist, National Interior Design Award
1991   RAIA Winner, Interior Architecture Award
          Light Makers Award Winner, Louis Poulsen

Exhibitions
1984   Architext Gallery, Melbourne
1986   RMIT Architecture Gallery, Melbourne
1992   Up Gallery, Melbourne
1994   Tolarno Galleries, Melbourne
          Museum of Victoria, Melbourne
1995   Gallery for Contemporary Art, Celje, Slovenia
1996   Models Inc Artists and Industry Gallery, Melbourne
          Architecture on the Horizon, Royal Institute
           of British Architects, London
1997   Interbuild, Sydney
          First and Third Generation Architects,
           University of Melbourne

Lectures
1993   Faculty of Environmental Design and Construction,
          RMIT
1994   Surround International Conference on Interior
          Architecture, Melbourne
1995   ID One Lecture Series, Melbourne
1996   W Lim and Associates, Singapore
          Workshop for Architecture and Urbanism, Tokyo
          Bartlett School of Architecture, London
1997   Designex, International Conference, Melbourne
          Morphe: 1997 Biennial Oceanic Architecture and
           Design Student Conference, Australia
          Royal Australian Institute of Architects, Sydney
          Art in Architecture, New Zealand Institute of Architects

Selected projects
1990   Squire Boutique, Melbourne
          The Cherry Tree, Melbourne
1991   Succhi, Melbourne
1993   Gan House, Melbourne
1994   Capitol, Melbourne
          Gibbs Church Conversion, Melbourne
1995   Curve Gallery, Melbourne
          Sapore Restaurant, Melbourne
          Ryan Studio, Melbourne
1996   Atlas House, Melbourne
          Urban Attitude, Melbourne
          Barkly Apartments, Melbourne
          Pless House, Melbourne
1997   Island House, Victoria
          Tonic, Sydney
          A'Beckett Student Housing, Melbourne
          Student Apartments, Melbourne
          Cinema Complex, Paris, France
          Apartments, Jaffa, Israel

Competitions
1994   Museum of Victoria, Melbourne – Tom Kovac in
          collaboration with Dennis Daniel, Colin Rofe, and
          Christy Mckanna
1996   Pontian Centre, Melbourne
          Federation Square, Melbourne – Tom Kovac and Geoff
           Malone in collaboration with Cassandra Fahey, Lim
           Chiauw, Paul Bavister and Atelier One, London
           (structural engineer)

Journal Articles

1990   Alex Selenitsch, 'Cherry Tree', *Interior Architecture*
        (Australia), January, pp122-31.
        Herbert Ypma, 'Altered Image', *Interior Architecture*
        (Australia), May, p34.
        'Cherry Tree Hotel', *Architecture Australia*
        (Australia), November, p57.

1991   John Andrews, 'Carved Space', *Architecture Australia*
        (Australia), March 1991, pp70-78.
        Shoichi Muto, 'Tom Kovac', *Wind* (Japan), Spring, pp38-43.
        Helen Fletcher, 'Succhi', *Interior Architecture* (Australia),
        June, pp110-13.
        Kristina Hampel, 'The Designer as on-Site Sculptor', *The
        Interior* (Australia), September/November, pp18-19.

1992   Herbert Ypma, 'Tom Kovac', *Interior Architecture*
        (Australia), March, p34.
        Peter Zellner, 'Australian Avant-Garde', *Tostem View*
        (Japan), May, pp42-50.
        Sy Chen, 'Sculptural Metaphors', *CIA News* (Japan),
        June, pp28-29.
        RAIA Editorial, 'Interior Awards', *Architect* (Australia),
        October, p46.
        Teruo Kurosaki, 'Tom Kovac', *Kukan* (Japan), November,
        pp64-74.

1993   Jackie Cooper/Shane Murray, 'Gan House', *Architecture
        Australia* (Australia), January/Febuary, p54.
        John Beckmann, 'Showrooms', *International
        Interiors*, (USA), Summer, pp108-109.
        Davina Jackson, 'Tom: Leuchtendes Beispeil', *Ambiente*
        (Germany), December, p44.

1995   Dale Jones-Evans, 'Fluid Grooves', *Architecture
        Australia* (Australia), January, pp38-41.
        Caroline Roux, 'Learning Curves', *Blueprint* (UK),
        February, p45.
        Graham Foreman, 'Capitol Club', *Monument*

(Australia), March, pp54-56.
        Penny Maguire, 'Melbourne Pulse', *The Architectural
        Review* (UK), May, pp79-81.
        Cath Lovitt, 'Surround – Tom Kovac', *The Interior*
        (Australia), Spring/Summer, pp24-25.
        Heidi Dokulil, 'Atlas House', *Monument* (Australia),
        October, p106.

1996   Heidi Dokulil, 'Pless House', *Monument* (Australia),
        January, p119.
        Beatte Bellman, 'Capitol', *Arkitecture Und Licht*
        (Germany), May.
        Anne Marie Kiely, 'Curved Ellipse', *Belle –
        Corporate/Office Design* (Australia), June pp36-41.
        Dale Jones-Evans/Leon van Schaik, on the work of
        Tom Kovac in: Architecture On The Horizon,
        Architectural Design Profile no 122 (UK),
        July/August, pp8-11.
        Marcus O'Donnell, 'Sapore', *Monument* (Australia),
        September, p85.
        Penny Mcguire, 'Sense and Sensuality', *The
        Architectural Review* (UK), November, pp88-89.
        Masaaki Takahashi, 'Interview with Tom Kovac', *Wind*
        (Japan), November, pp61-68.
        Doug Evans, 'The Secret Life of Contemporary
        Melbourne Architecture', *B, Architecture Journal*
        (Denmark), no 52/53, pp123-26.

1997   Leon van Schaik, 'Architect on the Horizon', *Monument*
        (Australia), February, p35.
        Leon van Schaik, 'Neither Carved Nor Moulded: An
        Architecture of the Third Term', Light in Architecture,
        Architectural Design Profile no 126 (UK),
        March/April, pp76-77.
        Aardvaark (RMIT Journal, Australia), 'Kovac
        Architecture', ppD4, F2, G9, G23, K8, K16.

1998   Masaaki Nakada, 'Tom Kovac', *A+U* (Japan), January.